THIN WHITE LINE

THIN WHITE LINE

Andy Cave

HUTCHINSON
LONDON

Published by Hutchinson 2008

2 4 6 8 10 9 7 5 3 1

Copyright © Andy Cave 2008

Andy Cave has asserted his right under the Copyright, Designs
and Patents Act 1988 to be identified as the author of this work

First published in Great Britain in 2008 by
Hutchinson
Random House, 20 Vauxhall Bridge Road, London SW1V 2SA

www.rbooks.co.uk

Addresses for companies within The Random House Group Limited can be found at:
www.randomhouse.co.uk/offices.htm

The Random House Group Limited Reg. No. 954009

A CIP catalogue record for this book
is available from the British Library

ISBN 9780091795726

Mixed Sources
Product group from well-managed
forests and other controlled sources
www.fsc.org Cert no. TT-COC-2139
© 1996 Forest Stewardship Council
FSC

The Random House Group Limited supports
the Forest Stewardship Council (FSC), the leading international forest certification
organisation. All our titles that are printed on Greenpeace approved FSC certified
paper carry the FSC logo. Our paper procurement policy can be found at
www.rbooks.co.uk/environment

Typeset in Garamond MT by Palimpsest Book Production Limited,
Grangemouth, Stirlingshire

Printed and bound in Great Britain by
Clays Ltd, St Ives plc

To Andy Parkin and Mick Fowler,
for reminding us all how to explore the
mountains with such commitment and integrity

Every man carries within himself a world made up of all that he has seen and loved . . . and it is to this world that he returns incessantly, though he may pass through, and seem to inhabit, a world quite foreign to it.

De Chateaubriand

Above, in the clear air and searching sunlight, we are afoot with the quiet gods, and men can know each other and themselves for what they are.

A.F. Mummery, 1894

Contents

Illustrations

Second section

The Duke of Abruzzi leads first ascent of Mount St Elias
(© *Royal Geographical Society, London, UK/The Bridgeman Art Library*)

Tlingit Indians, Yakutat (*Edmond Meany Collection no. 132, University of Washington Libraries, Special Collections Division*)

Bob Reeve (*University of Alaska Anchorage, Consortium Library, Archives & Special Collections*)

Mick Fowler meets a polar bear, Juneau airport, Alaska

Hubbard Glacier and Russell Fjord, St Elias Mountains, Alaska/Yukon

Kurt Gloyer (*Mick Fowler*)

Andy, Kurt and his Cessna (*Mick Fowler*)

North Buttress of Mount Kennedy

Day One: Andy climbing Mount Kennedy (*Mick Fowler*)

Mick heats his inner boot

Day Four: The end of the storm (*Mick Fowler*)

Andy with headwall above

Andy mixed-climbing in the black diorite band (*Mick Fowler*)

Mick leaves the fifth bivouac

Mick approaching the summit of Mount Kennedy

Andy and Mick on the summit

The team at base camp

Andy Selters (*Andy Selters*)

Bill Pilling (*Andy Selters*)

Andy climbing End of the Affair, Curbar, Derbyshire (*John Houlihan*)

Unless otherwise attributed, all photographs are from the author's collection

Maps

1

Gold-plated

Derbyshire, June 1997

I searched for a way across the stream. The stew-brown water gushed over rocks and then swerved down towards the bright green copse in the valley. Up above, I saw Elaine waiting at the plateau's edge. I stumbled across the wet rocks, my feet feeling wooden, froth sticking to the end of my boots. My thumb, frostbitten in the mountains, pulsed unremittingly. I hadn't wanted to do the walk, but as I reached her my mood lightened.

'Thanks for encouraging me to come up here,' I said, a little out of breath.

'Well done,' she said tenderly. 'It will probably do you the world of good.'

The high plateau of Kinder Scout rolled northwards, a maze of black mud avenues, crescents and dead ends that scurried around the tall bronze islands of heather.

We sat down, sipped water and listened to the plovers piping.

'You ever seen a short-eared owl?' I said.

'No, do you get them on Kinder?'

'They nest in the peat banks, somewhere around here they reckon.'

I remembered my first time on these moors as a fourteen-year-old, with the kids from back home. As soon as we got off the train, the twins had let Edale know that we were in town, scrawling 'Royston Skins Rule OK' in large black letters across the timetable posted on the platform. We'd gone straight to the pub, where Rhino had bought us a couple of pints each. Then we'd set off up here. Already bored with the outdoors, the twins had started throwing stones at the sheep. The cloud dropped suddenly. I got out my map, but the twins called me a gay boy, so I put it away again and we trudged over the moor for hours, disorientated, trying to find the northern edge by the Snake Pass Road. At the end of the day we peered down at a village, but it was Edale again; we had walked in a complete circle.

Today it was clear, but it was easy to see how people got lost and why so many planes had crashed over the years. The moor was often shrouded in mist and it was the highest land mass for miles. You came across relics sometimes, dull silver shrapnel in the skin of the black peat.

Elaine and I shared a passion for wild places, but I always preferred a challenge at the end of it. She loved the mountains too, but hated getting cold, frightened. She didn't need to push herself to the edge physically and psychologically, and I respected that.

'I'll make a walker out of you one day,' she joked as we set off back down.

At home that afternoon I cursed as the shoelace slipped through my hand for the third time. I was already late. Making knots was how I earned my living in the mountains, and now I couldn't tie two damn strands of string into a bow. I bent over and pulled the laces as tight as I could with my teeth, and then, with the unbandaged hand, stuffed the excess down between my shoe and sock.

At the doctor's surgery I sat and waited my turn next to an older woman wearing a hat and a thick woollen overcoat. What a ridiculous outfit to wear on such a beautiful summer's day, I thought, as she talked on and on about her illnesses and then her husband's, all the time staring hard at the bandage on my hand, desperate to know what misfortune had occurred.

Her conversation was dull, but it distracted me from what lay ahead, from what the doctor might decide was best, and I was grateful to her for that.

Finally, unable to hold back any longer, she asked, 'What have you done to your thumb, duck?'

It didn't seem appropriate to explain, sitting there below the verdant, modest hills of the Pennines, and so I lied, or tried to: 'I was putting a picture up on the wall and . . .'

But she was off again: 'Oh dear, my son did that not so long back. Terrible, it was. Swelled up like a balloon.'

At that moment the buzzer sounded, providing me with a timely escape.

The possible treatment options I'd read about varied wildly from straightforward amputation to bathing in whirlpools. One approach sounded particularly gruesome:

If you do not have antibiotics and the frostbite wound has become severely infected, does not heal, and ordinary debridement is impossible, consider maggot therapy, despite its hazards:

- *Expose the wound to flies for one day and then cover it.*
- *Check daily for maggots.*
- *Once maggots develop, keep wound covered but check daily.*
- *Remove all maggots when they have cleaned out all dead tissue and before they start on healthy tissue. Increased pain and bright red blood in the wound indicate that the maggots have reached healthy tissue.*
- *Flush the wound repeatedly with sterile water or fresh urine to remove the maggots.*
- *Check the wound every four hours for several days to ensure all maggots have been removed.*

As the nurse carefully unwound the bandage the doctors in Delhi had put on, I looked away. The thumb had been black to begin with, then had turned green and started to smell. I joked about using maggots, trying to sound relaxed as I screwed my eyes shut and tensed my stomach.

She laughed. 'We don't have any maggots, I'm afraid,' she said, dropping the bandage into the bin, along with my detached thumbnail. 'But we've got this silver nitrate cream, typically used for severe burns. It's a magic cure for gangrene.'

She was gently cleaning the disfigured thumb when the doctor walked in.

'How're you doing?'

He was a big, friendly man with no hint of annoyance that a reckless mountaineer was taking up so much of the surgery's time; I suppose frostbite in the Peak District was a novelty at any time of the year. He had a reputation for being pretty adventurous himself, having allegedly crash-landed his gyro-copter in a nearby field, demolishing a stone wall and smashing himself up.

'We need to change the dressing every couple of days, and once the antibiotics take hold things will look much better,' reassured the nurse.

'Good. That's great,' he said, interested and calm.

'You don't appreciate how much you need thumbs until . . .' I ventured.

'That's right,' he said, then, after a pause, 'Where the hell have you been anyhow?'

'A mountain called Changabang in India,' I muttered.

'Did you get any good photos?'

I was glad he said this just then, as I didn't want to talk about the rest of it: the hunger, the tragedy, and the struggle to survive.

'Yes, some of them are stunning.'

'You'll have to come over for a drink one night and show them. I would imagine it's quite something out there.'

'Yes,' I said. 'It's another world entirely.'

A few nights later, the pain in my feet woke me. Since returning from India they had been numb, and I thought this was the result of repeatedly smashing my crampons against the ice. Whatever it was, the pain was unbearable, like hot barbed nails being driven through the soles of my feet and then yanked back out. The problem was that when the pain came, I couldn't sleep, and I started to think about things. It wasn't so bad during the day, but at night, when it was dark, it was harder to shut the demons out. I remembered the enormous avalanche powering down and sweeping my friend Brendan to his death. The rest of us had battled for three more days, crossing two 6000-metre cols. I arrived back at base camp after 17 days away; our friends Roger and Julie-Ann had virtually given us up for dead. Having survived towards the end with virtually no food, we were emaciated and had boils on our necks.

My thumb was much better now, and I didn't want to go and bother the doctor again. The feet looked fine, that was the strange thing, but the cold must have damaged something invisible to the naked eye.

Eventually, I went back to the surgery.

'I saw a young footballer in the winter. He suffered terrible circulation problems when training in the cold and we gave him some medication. I can't guarantee anything, but it worked for him.'

'What does it do?'

'It's been used for people with Raynaud's syndrome. In theory, it will dramatically improve the circulation.'

'I'll try anything: the pain seems to be getting worse rather than better.'

As summer slid by, my thumb gradually recovered, a new, pink skin emerged, and the miracle drugs helped to thaw out my feet and ease the pain. But inside I still felt numb, as if a thick glass screen lay between me and the world. Often I just wanted to be alone. Some days I avoided emails and ignored the telephone.

I didn't see the doctor socially for a while, but then he and his wife invited Elaine and me over to their house just before Christmas. The wine flowed and various local issues were scrutinised; then suddenly a lively discussion began about the perils of radon gas. Though more common in the villages of south Derbyshire, we learned that it had been detected in some homes around our village. Allegedly one woman had died of lung cancer a few miles away as a result of excess radon levels in her living room. In American homes, just 10 per cent of the UK level is considered unacceptable. Marvellous, I thought. I survive working underground in a coal mine and climbing in the rarefied air of the Himalayas, only to be ravaged by radon gas whilst watching the football in my front room.

'More wine?' said the doctor. 'Did I tell you about our trip to the Isle of Skye?'

I shook my head.

'Well, I've got a share in a small plane. I flew up with my friend Colin for the weekend and we climbed the Inaccessible Pinnacle. It was bloody brilliant,' he enthused, his eyes alight. 'When we came to leave, the winds were terrible, and it's only a makeshift airstrip at Glen Brittle.'

'I didn't realise there was an airstrip at Glen Brittle. I mean, there's nothing there.'

'Exactly. It's basically the beach. It was frightening, I can tell you. I thought we might be stranded, and it's the furthest I've ever flown in that plane.'

'It sounds insane.'

'By the way, I wanted to ask you: I fancy doing the Old Man of Hoy, off Orkney. Do you think someone of my limited experience could climb that?'

'I've not seen you climb.'

'We could take the plane up there for the weekend.'

'Fly to Hoy? Why? There's nowhere to land.'

'Why? Are *you* seriously asking me why?'

There was a noticeable silence, and then he began laughing.

'I never expected someone like you to ask me why I am doing something adventurous.'

I smiled and shrugged my shoulders.

Lying in bed later that night, I reflected on my words. Had I turned my back on adventure? If that conversation with the doctor had done anything, it had filled me with nostalgia.

I remembered that I, too, had been in Glen Brittle on the Isle of Skye, in February a few years earlier. It was the very first time that Mick Fowler and I climbed together.

'Andrew, we have excellent winter conditions,' he claimed, the morning we crawled out of the small tent pitched by the side of the road.

For Mick there had been a day in the Inland Revenue office, followed by a round-up of recruits, a seven-hour drive, a lecture in Glencoe, and then, because of the dangerous amounts of snow there, a further three-hour drive to Skye. After two days of pioneering first ascents, he would then drive all the way home, without any sleep whatsoever, change back into his suit and sit down at his tax office desk. This indefatigable enthusiasm and constant energy had become legendary; the BBC had even made a film about one of these eccentric, exhilarating weekends. For my part, I'd been guiding in the mountains of Glencoe all week, and would be doing so again the following week.

After half a cup of lukewarm tea and two slices of bread, smeared thickly with margarine, we set off walking through the magnificent Sron na Ciche corrie and up to the crest of the Cuillin by Sgurr Mhic Choinnich. I donned ski goggles in order to cope with the increasing wind and stinging snow. Having more sense, our friends Crags and Danuska, legendary for their stoicism, retreated to the valley. We descended steeply eastwards until we were beneath a formidable 600-foot black wall, a vague intermittent line of snow and ice running up its left side. For seven hours we scratched and clawed our way up this precarious ground with the tips of our ice axes and crampons.

'This is a brilliant climb,' I yelled down to Mick, after a particularly steep section.

On the summit, a storm-force wind tried to rip us from the slope and then battered us all the way back to Glen Brittle, where after only a few minutes Mick announced the outline for the rest of the weekend. 'We can sleep here again tonight and then do another route tomorrow. What do you think?'

'I'm keen to climb tomorrow, but what about food and a pint?' I smiled. 'I could murder a drink, and my clothes could do with drying out as well.'

His silence made me think I'd made unreasonable requests.

'I've got food here,' Mick said.

'What, precisely?'

'Bread, plenty of marg and some crisps, I think.'

I was flabbergasted. We had eaten bread and margarine for breakfast, climbed non-stop for 14 hours and, I guessed, used in excess of 7000 calories. I wouldn't have minded if it had been decent bread, but it was the whitest, thinnest stuff available; paper masquerading as food. I had spent much of the previous year living in the Basque country, a land where people adored food. Even when climbing in the mountains, the Basques ate like kings: tortillas, jamon, bacalao. Mick was clearly not a lover of food: for him, it was a fuel you had to consume, almost an inconvenience. His idea of haute cuisine was a Fray Bentos pie, and he'd once confessed that when his wife went away for a week, she simply left him seven tins, one for each day. Mick would pour water on cornflakes if milk was short and barely notice the difference.

'A rib-eye steak, followed by crumble and custard and then a few ales was more what I had in mind,' I ventured. 'Maybe a wee dram to finish.'

'It has snowed a lot during the day. Look at the road. I'm not sure we'd make it up the hill.'

'Well let's try it. I'm starving.'

Halfway up the hill, the car came to a halt, the wheels spinning belligerently in the snow.

'Why don't you and Crags go and sit on the bonnet. Some extra weight over the wheels might do it,' Mick suggested.

We duly perched with our legs dangling in front of the lights. Behind the icy windscreen Mick grinned, relishing the challenge. The car drifted left and right, creeping forward painfully slowly over the steepest part of the hill. But I got my steak and crumble, and the following day we climbed another superb new route.

Now, lying in bed, I knew something had changed even if I couldn't see how. A few weeks earlier Mick had asked me to join him in attempting an unclimbed mountain face in Peru, but although I had always dreamed of visiting the Andes, right now I lacked the desire. I couldn't stomach the thought of it. Mick, on the other hand, like the rest of the Changabang team, had turned his focus back to extreme mountaineering without hesitation. Steve Sustad had already returned to the mountains, to the formidable north face of Jannu in Nepal. Roger Payne and Julie-Ann Clyma were hoping to visit China later in the summer, and Mick had countless plans. Why did I feel different?

Our Changabang ascent in India had just been nominated for the Piolet d'Or award by the French, and I'd been invited to a formal ceremony in Chamonix. Countless thoughts crowded into my mind simultaneously, until I couldn't lie still any more. I went downstairs, poured myself a large whisky, threw another chunk of wood on the fire and sprawled out along the settee. I had been offered a few days of work in Chamonix ski-guiding, and the money would be useful. I might as well attend the ceremony.

All day snow fell like feathers, until the only colour left in the town was white, milk white, over pavements, cars, trees, hats and hair. In the evening it continued, a slow descent, graceful and noiseless, so that with closed eyes the only sensation was a gentle tickle and burn as the flakes slid from your cheeks. It was as if the snow normally reserved for high summits had become lost and decided to rest here on the street. At the hotel, the door was shut tight, locked. Through the square of the window I watched leather and fur mingling by the bar, the dazzle of lights on glass, and rows of waiting plates crammed with untouched food. I knocked at the door. No answer. I stared in at the warmth and splendour of the room again and noticed a cameraman striding around, capturing the fizz of it all for French TV. I knocked again, but again no reply.

A couple appeared. They too walked up to the door and knocked. Perhaps it was a secret Masonic knock, as the door opened. I rushed in behind them.

'Ticket?' a woman asked curtly. No one had told me I needed a ticket, and before I had time to formulate a response in French, she slammed the door shut.

I noticed a poster on the back of the door partially covered in snow, advertising the evening – 'Piolet d'Or, 7 Fevrier 1998, Hotel Arbatte, Chamonix-Mt-Blanc'. The main body of the poster was a photograph of a mountaineer perched dramatically on a vertical piece of blue ice in the Himalayas, thousands of feet off the ground. I wiped snow from the poster with the sleeve of my jacket and looked more closely: it was, in fact, me.

The Piolet d'Or is recognised as the most prestigious mountaineering award in the world, and to be nominated it must mean that in the eyes of the judges, our team had achieved something special. The annual award, given by *Montagnes* magazine and the French mountaineering organisation, the Groupe de Haute Montagne, attempts to reward the most significant ascent of the year. Ideally the ascent captures the true spirit of alpinism, demonstrating extreme technical difficulty, psychological commitment and innovative approach whilst retaining respect for the mountains. In a sense it gives a message to the mountaineering community, declaring what the sponsors and the jury consider to be the essence of alpinism. It is the nearest thing mountaineering has to the Oscars. For many mountaineers such an idea is ridiculous. How can trophies be awarded for such an arbitrary activity? Of course some people like tables and values, and endeavour to measure everything in the world no matter how pointless. Such a system works well for sports like athletics or skiing, and has some success in recognising the achievements of rock-climbers, but in the high mountains, ever-changing conditions and unpredictable weather render the idea of objective measurement absurd. Indeed, the idea of a committee comparing one ascent with another and handing out an ice axe covered in gold paint to the 'best' has been thought so ridiculous by some top mountaineers that they have boycotted the event.

The cold had got into my feet now and I wished I had been more assertive with the woman at the door. Fortunately, just then the curly hair and wide shoulders of Stevie Haston appeared, his partner Laurence at his side. I explained my sorry predicament.

'Bunch of fucking idiots, the lot of them,' he declared unequivocally.

'It's so stupid. You are the one giving a talk, no?' Laurence said.

If Stevie couldn't get me in, nobody could. A phenomenal alpinist now living in Chamonix, he was something of a mythical figure in climbing circles, someone who featured as the central character in a number of outrageous stories, both in and out of the mountains. A recent one on the circuit centred around an overzealous Italian mountain rescue team mistakenly trying to rescue him. After much confusion, shouting and a scuffle in the snow, Stevie had sauntered past them back to the valley.

Stevie had been reared in a tough East End area of London and spent his spare time Thai boxing. With all these tales, actual details and motivations get lost, but essentially they end with an authoritarian figure, or someone trying to impose regulations, being humiliated. Anyhow, the fact that we found ourselves inside the Piolet d'Or event within a few seconds was not a surprise, tickets or no tickets.

Clusters of well-known French alpinists stood chatting, drinking, lean and athletic, people I had only ever seen before in climbing films or magazines. The only people I actually knew were a group of Slovenian friends who had positioned themselves right next to the free wine; an impressive stack of Côtes-du-Rhône that stretched towards the ceiling. Stevie, Laurence and I went to sit with them. As one of the nominees for the award, I knew that I would have to go up on stage and describe our climb, and so I drank to overcome my fear of speaking to a huge crowd of relative strangers.

'*Excusez-moi*, Andy. Would it mean a lot for your team to win the Piolet d'Or award?' asked Jean-Marc, a reporter from *Montagnes* magazine.

The wine had already taken a firm grip of me and I hadn't given thought to the questions I was likely to be asked. I was proud of what we had achieved on Changabang, though desperately sad about what had happened during the descent. Although the climb had come to an end, its effects were still with me. What a group of arbitrary individuals fuelled by financial and media interest thought of it would not make a huge difference to our opinion. Why people climb cannot be reduced to simple answers. Why people climb in the extreme environment of the Himalayas proves even more difficult to justify. The battle in mountaineering is often a battle with the self, a private affair, yourself and a friend working as a team to unlock the mountain's secret; a world beyond speed records and judges, rules and spectators, a quirky activity where you don't normally receive material accolades, only occasional admiration from climbing peers. Only these people, even if they have never set foot in the Himalayas, can understand what motivates someone to give total emotional, physical and financial commitment to an ultimately pointless activity.

'I don't really mind,' I said, speaking from the heart, looking straight at him and trying to ignore the camera to the right.

Up on the stage, someone addressed the crowd, explaining the history of the award and then inviting up Marko Prezelj and Andrej Štremfelj. They had won the very first Piolet d'Or back in 1991 for a remarkable ascent on Kanchenjunga. Considered two of the world's best alpinists, they looked embarrassed and in broken English mumbled something into the microphone before returning to their table to carry on drinking.

The representatives from the five nominated groups were now invited in turn to describe their ascents. I had drunk nothing but red wine for two hours, and by the time I climbed up on to the stage, the whole room had began to sway as if I was balancing on a rocking chair. I decided to make my statements as brief as possible.

Turning, I saw myself projected on to the wall. I had worried that seeing scenes from the Changabang climb might upset me, but instead I felt detached. I stared in awe at the image of me poised on thin ice. It was as if the figures in that vertical frozen landscape were strangers. Yet despite the wine, I knew the script, and I stumbled through, dry-mouthed. I showed only five shots, as planned. I hadn't the strength to describe the descent in detail and how it had all gone wrong on day 12.

The greatest personal loss was the knowledge that our beautiful climb and all the combined effort in achieving it could never be relived over a pint, as it should have been. Standing on the stage only compounded this terrible loneliness. Deep down I knew that sooner or later I would need to ask fundamental questions of myself. Mountains had been the bedrock of my existence, but now something felt different. Would I ever regain the nerve to tackle such an audacious climb again? Was I frightened of returning and failing? And perhaps most important of all, did I care about climbing mountains any more?

'Hey, how's it going, kid?' Andy Parkin thrust out his hand. The legendary alpinist and artist had been based in Chamonix for over 15 years, but he'd lost none of his Sheffield accent and none of his vitality.

'I'm knackered. I'm leaving. I'm supposed to be skiing tomorrow.'

'So the Russians won it for their route on Makalu. Bit of a shame, kid. Never mind the ice axe; the cash is useful,' he said, his dazzling silk shirt unbuttoned halfway down his chest. 'There's another do tomorrow night if you fancy it. More local trophies for the French. They love this stuff. There'll be a decent buffet, too.'

Pushing the door open, I stepped outside. The snow had stopped, and high on the mountain a light from a ski station shone brightly. It was a beautiful night, and tomorrow there would be some great skiing in the trees.

2

Embers

The following summer, I saw Andy Parkin outside his studio in Les Praz, staring up at the Chamonix Aiguilles. His deep, almost mystical relationship with mountains set him apart from most other climbers I knew. The previous week he had vanished into the mountains alone, spying out a new line on the giant north face of the Grande Jorrasses. At night he had slept in a tiny forgotten bivouac shelter perched 2000 feet above the Mallet Glacier. During the day, when not scanning the face with binoculars, he searched for crystals or set up his easel and painted. Often, I thought that this intense relationship he had with the natural world was what sustained him in life, the slender thread that kept him from falling into darkness following his accident.

Earlier, up high, a gentle breeze had kept me cool, but down in the valley the air stood still, hot and dry, like desert air. I parked my car and walked over. I was working as a mountain guide and staying at Andy's apartment further up the valley.

'Hey. How was it up there?'

'Pleasant but busy,' I said, aware that I had interrupted something.

'Sure, this is the busiest week of the summer. It's the Fête des Guides. I went into town to do some chores but it's insane down there.'

On a makeshift table beside him lay pieces of coloured broken glass. On the grass sat a twisted sheet of brass and alongside it a length of thick wire. I remembered him saying that the brass had once formed part of an ancient mountain refuge before it fell on to the glacier, which had chewed and torn at it before spewing it on to the moraine decades later. The wire came from an old *téléphérique* cable that had lain abandoned in the forest. Inside his studio these metals would be moulded and soldered into art: a wire figure skiing; a piece of brass that looked like a horse's chest. Unwanted mountain detritus salvaged and sculpted to make people think about the world differently.

'For a guy in Switzerland, those,' he said. 'Commissions.'

Ironically, the long path that had led him to painting and to soldering brass and copper together to produce art here in Chamonix had begun once he had abandoned his apprenticeship in the steel city of Sheffield, his home town. After travelling and climbing around the world, he had moved out here, washing dishes at night and climbing during the day. Eventually the opportunity to work unofficially as a mountain guide arose and, desperate for cash, he took it. One day in Switzerland, he was lowering his two clients down to a ledge when the belay ripped from the rock. Almost down on to the safety of the ledge, the clients fell a relatively short distance. Inescapably, their weight on the rope came immediately and violently on to Andy, tearing him from his stance. He survived the huge fall, but in the helicopter on the way to the hospital his heart stopped. He was revived, but again it stopped. Somehow, to the amazement of the medics, he survived.

He never spoke about the accident itself, but he talked openly about how he had rediscovered a latent talent for art and how it had saved him. His skill and vision as an artist had manifested itself when he was a child, but it took this near escape from death to rouse his full potential.

'Until then I was too busy climbing. Suddenly, that was the end of that. Then me and the girlfriend split up. I lost everything. The art was a kind of therapy, I guess.'

Following years of surgery, one hip fused rigidly and an elbow permanently fixed in a position of ninety degrees, he returned to the mountains with vigour. He rarely complained and never used his disability as an excuse, and because he was such a talented climber, you tended to forget about these lingering injuries. Since the accident, he had established many of the most difficult mixed climbs in the Mont Blanc massif, if not the whole of the Alps, linking together previously unthought-of ephemeral slivers of ice, a feat for anyone in the face of the competitive local scene. I had climbed a short new route with him one winter and was awestruck by the resourcefulness and skill with which he had developed highly personalised techniques of movement. On expeditions to the Himalayas, Andy was always trying to break new ground. On K2 he'd attempted a first ascent; on Everest he had climbed without oxygen. These were outings you couldn't hire a local guide for; they were just too hard and too risky.

Andy rented a small apartment and didn't own a car. I detected a quest for a pure, uncluttered ideal in his life; something that resonated in his approach to climbing as well as in his work as an artist.

'I might wander back and get a shower. Do you want a lift?'

'No thanks. I'll be back soon.'

I crossed the meadow, left my boots to dry by the door and went inside. Andy's apartment was a modest but welcoming place. Next to the small gas stove sat a tiny sink, in the corner was a plain glass-fronted wood-burning stove and in the centre a round table with four chairs. By the door stood an old hi-fi, and there was plenty of jazz and rows of books on everything from the night sky to impressionism, from Dickens to Sartre. And stuff everywhere, stuff full of meaning: feathers, crystals, carved pieces of wood; scraps of paper with sketched faces, miniature works of genius, examinations of people and the masks they wore. It was clearly not the home of a poor man; there was little of any monetary value and yet it had incredible charm, something that couldn't be bought, objects that could be assembled only by living a certain life, reminders of extraordinary journeys made.

Standing on the worktop was a mountain stove that Andy had adapted by adding super-lightweight wires so that it could be hung from inside a tent or from a piton. A piece of copper from the burner wrapped around the tiny gas bottle, conducting heat and making the machine much more efficient in the cold. He had turned an average bit of kit into something quite brilliant. Beside it was his legendary flask, a battered thing with a rough piece of cork as a lid that he filled with a curious homemade herbal brew and honey when venturing into the mountains.

I put on some water for tea and then scoured his books, my fingers resting on one by Padre Alberto de Agostini. I lifted the heavy volume on to the couch. The cover reminded me of the books that sat in the basements of university libraries, lonely books that slowly collected dust. The name Agostini sounded familiar, or was I thinking of Abruzzi, the Italian mountaineering aristocrat? I began staring at the extraordinary photographs inside and sensed magic. I found an image of kind but serious-looking priests in formal religious attire. Next was a photograph of two men dressed in ancient aviator jackets, standing next to a single-propeller aeroplane. The plane had been set down, rather improbably, on a rough piece of grass in front of an enormous lake. A few miles away a ranch sat at the water's edge; behind it a plain stretched away before butting into a cluster of glaciated peaks. Agostini had his hands in his pockets; the other man was a legendary pioneering Andean pilot named Franco Bianco, from Italy. In another photo, Agostini, dressed in old mountaineering garb, was standing on the summit of San Lorenzo between two European guides, an Argentinian flag flapping in the wind. A beautiful, eerie image of Fitzroy appeared next. It was a simple, uncluttered portrait of the mighty peak, tinged green by the printing process. A few pages further on, and a dozen slender trees huddled together, compact, resolute, every branch bent aggressively to the right by the dominant south-west wind.

It looked more like something a cartoonist might conjure, an exaggeration, a caricature of a windswept land. I hadn't felt my heart race on turning the pages of a book since first discovering the books of Walter Bonatti and Gaston Rebuffat as a teenager. The flicker of romance and the visual suggestion of a world unknown ignited fire in my chest.

The room had filled with steam. I jumped up, turned off the gas and returned to the book. The extraordinary range of photographs was bewildering. Here was an Italian missionary priest who climbed mountains, flew around in aeroplanes and made ethnographic records of local Indian tribes. He had penetrated into the mountainous heart of Patagonia, much further and deeper than either Magellan and Darwin before him or Chatwin and Theroux afterwards. Exhilarated, I laid the book down on the table and took a beer from the fridge. I was fascinated by this remote landscape and inspired by Agostini's sense of adventure.

I remembered then the significance of the name. I had once been invited on an expedition to climb Mount Sarmiento, a peak in Tierra del Fuego, in the extreme south of Patagonia. Agostini had organised the expedition that made the first ascent of the mountain in the 1950s. I had declined the invitation mainly because I was obsessed with exploring the Himalayas, and the modest heights of Patagonian summits hadn't seemed worthy of my interest. Looking at Agostini's photographs now, I felt the allure of the south.

Patagonia had always seemed to be a land shrouded in myth, a place full of strange encounters. Written accounts by travellers to the region simply reinforced the idea that it was a place of peculiar happenings. Magellan's men had survived by consuming boiled leather, rats and sawdust. The Frenchman Guinnard had been captured by local Indians and enslaved for three years. Certain Indian tribes used dogs to catch fish. Even Butch Cassidy and the Sundance Kid had spent time robbing banks there.

The door opened. I jumped. It was Andy. I realised that I had been staring at the book for hours.

'Padre de Agostini: quite a good book that,' he said, throwing his jacket on to a chair.

'It's an amazing book. Obviously a very adventurous guy.'

'Oh yes. You've not been down south, have you?'

'No. I don't think I've ever been past the equator, come to think of it.'

'Well there's plenty to do down there. You eaten?'

'Not yet. I didn't know if you fancied going out.' I was ravenous.

'I want to go out for a beer, but there's food here. I'm going to get a shower first.'

Whenever I looked in Andy's cupboards, I struggled to find anything obvious to eat: almost empty jars of herbs, a bag of rice, a few lentils. He owned a curious collection of pans and crockery, too. It might be best if he cooked: he knew his own kitchen.

'So you haven't been to Patagonia? That's uncanny,' he said, emerging from his bedroom, towel-drying his long hair.

'It's been a while since I went away on a big adventure anywhere.'

'I know. After your trip to Changabang, it will take time to heal. You'll return to the big mountains, but only when it feels right.'

'Maybe Patagonia is the place.'

'You need time down south. It's essential. You can't rush it, because of the weather. I mean, you might get lucky but you need patience.'

'Dave Hesleden is keen to do a trip somewhere. Is there much new stuff to do? Not too difficult?'

After a remarkably tasty casserole, created from the contents of the empty-looking cupboards, Andy began unearthing photos and route diagrams on scraps of paper from a huge wooden chest. His erratic filing system made mine look as meticulous as the British Library.

'The west face of Fitzroy – now that's a big challenge, still not climbed in alpine style.' He traced a knife across a black-and-white print of a steep mountain face. 'This is a good place, too. We went up here and then I stayed on and climbed this line here.' The point of the knife rested on a vertical shield of rock perhaps 2000 feet high, smothered with snow and ice, easing a little only towards the top.

'Jesus, who did you climb that with? It looks desperate.'

'The other guy had to leave, so I climbed solo.'

I was shocked. 'You went up there alone?'

He started to laugh.

'Did you use a rope as a backup, in case you fell?'

'No, nothing. I mean, I like to climb in good style, right?'

'It looks crazy.'

'I had a moment, mind you. My ice tool ripped and then the second one started to slip. Just there.' He pointed halfway up the face with the tip of the knife. 'It's the closest I've ever been to properly blowing it, I reckon.'

I was intrigued that he chose the word 'properly', as if there was any other way you could blow such a situation. There was little to add. He had soloed many hard climbs, and so if he had found it as challenging as anything he had previously achieved, further qualification was irrelevant. After almost two hours of staring at photos and chatting, I felt exhausted.

'I've seen enough. Let's go for that drink.'

We walked into town. It was a beautiful still evening, and warm, Mont Blanc a pale outline against a deepening blue sky towering above the town. We sat on the terrace, short-sleeved, sipping Kilkenny.

'The French are discovering real ale, finally. London Pride, Boddingtons.'

'There'll be a fish and chip shop soon,' I said.

'Well, you never know.'

'You got any big trips lined up?'

'There's talk of Shishapangma in Tibet. Victor reckons he knows somebody that might want to fund the trip. I mean, otherwise it's impossible. The Chinese government want so much money for the climbing permit these days.'

'Which face would that be?'

'The south face – you know, the steep side. And of course we want to try it in winter. It's not been done before.'

When Andy spoke, the world became a place of limitless possibilities. The range and scope of his ideas was endless. He had imagination, combined with extraordinary self-belief, expertise and tenacity. Beer cost twice the price as it did in Britain, but it slipped down easily enough as Andy spoke of his bold plans for Tibet. He was in his late forties, and yet his thirst for adventure was undiminished.

'That guy Agostini must have been one hell of an explorer,' I said, harking back to my earlier thoughts.

'Not half. Climbing San Lorenzo sixty years ago.'

'I love that book.'

'It's rare, you know. Cost me a fortune. I'm desperate to get down south again, but next time I want to go far south, Tierra del Fuego. The light down there for painting is something else. You need a boat, for sure. It's where Tilman ended up.'

'His photos are incredible too.'

'He would have been inspired by Vittoria Sella, the amazing Italian photographer who travelled with the Duke of Abruzzi on Mount St Elias, up in Alaska. Some of Agostini's shots, around Fitzroy and the Patagonian ice cap, were taken from an aeroplane. In fact he nearly made the first crossing of the ice cap. Tilman did it in the end.'

How strange, I thought, that we had separately abandoned council estates in steel and coal towns to wash up here in Chamonix chatting about the ends of the earth. Was it pure chance, or was there something working inside us beyond our control, an inquisitive gene, a desire to keep turning over stones?

'You should get yourself to Patagonia.'

'The last time you went, on Cerro Torre, didn't you have an epic?'

'Well it was a bit crazy, that one.' He started laughing.

'What was the problem?'

'The climbing was excellent; hard, but good. But then the

storm hit and we weren't sure how far the summit was. It got serious. The wind was crazy. We just had to get down. And then of course the food ran out and we were out on the ice cap for days. We found some berries to eat. Without them I don't know what would have happened.'

'You seem to live on nuts and berries anyhow, Andy,' I joked.

I was about to go to the bar for one more drink when John Whittle and Russell Brice appeared. John had smooth silver hair, a sharp mind and a generous laugh. I had served part of my apprenticeship as a mountain guide under his supervision and had been impressed by his skill and speed in the high mountains. Most of all, though, I enjoyed his sense of fun, and his ability to see the absurdity in everyday life. A Kiwi, Russell was famous for his prowess at high altitude and his outstanding organisational skills. These talents had allowed him to take countless clients to the summit of Everest. Climbing aside, it was his extraordinary capacity for beer that impressed us most.

As subtle as a dour farmer bidding at a cattle market, he raised his hand fleetingly to summon a barmaid to our table with two large jugs of beer. The term 'being Russelled' had recently entered the lexicon of English-speaking mountain guides to describe the concept of a quick drink escalating into something prodigious. We chinked our glasses.

Soon a whole series of outlandish tales began. It had been a while since I'd laughed so much, and it reminded me of the special bond between climbers. Like the men I had worked with at the coal mine, the dangerous day-to-day living engendered a special sense of camaraderie.

I hadn't noticed any hand movements from Russell, but suddenly two more jugs of beer appeared.

'You've been to Patagonia, haven't you, John?'

'Yes. Long time ago now, though. We were just one rope-length away from making the first ascent of Cerro Standhart.'

'What stopped you?'

'The weather.'

'Andy's been getting me inspired.'

'The thing I remember down there is the wind. I was picked up and carried through the air.'

'Honestly?' I said. John was a big, solidly built man.

'Yes. Where else do you get winds that carry men? A skinny bugger like you has got no chance.'

I had to work the next day and it was getting raucous. I was enjoying the banter, but after one more glass I excused myself and walked back, thinking of Patagonia the whole way. The photos in Agostini's book had inspired me, stirring my imagination for the first time since returning from India. I was starting to feel fit and strong again too, after guiding all summer in the mountains. Perhaps I was ready to return to the bigger mountains and try something for myself again.

The following morning I woke early and staggered into the kitchen. Something hard struck my shins and I fell forward with an almighty crash on to a pile of sharp, hard junk.

'What the hell,' I muttered.

The entire kitchen was full of bent copper piping, splintered wood and rusting steel bars. I found out later that Andy had found the stuff on a demolition site on his way back from the bar in the middle of the night and had decided to make numerous shuttle carries. I couldn't face breakfast. I packed my rucksack, grabbed my boots and headed out for a coffee.

In town, the local mountain guides were getting ready for their annual parade up to the church, where they had their ice axes blessed and welcomed the newly qualified young guides, as well as paying respects to those who had died. For men and women who spent so much time away from friends and family in the high mountains, it provided an opportunity to celebrate their shared lives and fate, giving them pride, confidence and hope.

I met my clients at the Montenvers funicular train station. I explained that the exercise of the day was to go up on to the Mer de Glace and learn how to walk in crampons and use an ice axe. It was basic stuff but vital for secure, efficient movement on a mountain. I would also show them how to travel safely across glaciers, so that one day they would feel confident venturing out themselves, without fear of lurking crevasses. I always looked forward to these days, watching clients progress rapidly from their initial clumsiness to a point where they felt as if the spikes on the soles of their feet had been there for ever and the ice axe was a simple extension of their arm.

The engine of the train strained as we pulled up steeply through the forest, the smell of pine needles and diesel wafting through the carriage. It was strange, but each time I took this train I found myself reliving early climbing adventures. I smiled, remembering Terry dropping his rucksack on the Bonatti Pillar. It was my first time on the mountain and we had been up near the summit. Another memory of the Dru sprouted from the first.

Dave Hesleden and I had only just started climbing in the mountains together, and the Dru Couloir Direct was our first route. I recalled the colour of the ice as we finally left the shade, the angle easing, the sun making everything sparkle. We smiled, enjoying that moment immediately before the summit, easy but special. Though her face looked good, lightning strikes had torn holes in the alloy at the back of the Madonna's head. That didn't add up somehow; if the statue of the Virgin had been attacked, what hope was there for us?

A few hours below the summit, we found a small hole in the ice, crawled in and slept, starting again at first light. At the shoulder two men waved and called. Something looked wrong. They were new to the game, I could tell; out of breath and with their slings all tangled, but it wasn't that. Their eyes flickered restlessly and they pointed to a tiny dark speck on the glacier below.

'We heard a scream. There might have been an avalanche.' The first man spoke in staccato, each word a bullet. 'We met a guy in the hut last night, a Geordie bloke, nice, by himself. He was going up there somewhere.'

The other man nodded nervously; he was overdressed, and in the full sun, his head dripped with sweat.

Knowing the way meant we travelled fast, but it was 2000 feet, steep and exposed, and it still took us well over an hour to reach the glacier. We tied into the rope and started weaving through the chaos of ice, teetering across snow bridges. Once through the icefall, we headed straight down, searching for the speck.

'Over there, Andy,' said Dave.

I saw the body and my heart started hammering. He lay face down, steam rising from his neck, warm. I looked but I didn't want to.

'Dave, mate, run to the hut. Get a chopper. You're faster than me.'

At the coal mine I'd been a first-aider, but I had never had to do it for real. A ring, tattoos, jet-black hair. Somebody. A good bloke, a Geordie; I'd met them before. Made the world go round. Salt of the earth. Fucking hell.

Pulse.

'Hello. My name's Andy. Can you hear me?'

Wrist. Neck. Chest. Nothing. Fuck. No breath.

He'd been there for hours, I realised. Every finger was swollen, like ripe black grapes. The chopper pilot arrived, hovered and with a circling motion of his hand gesticulated – wrap the sling around his waist, then clip. How do you know he's dead? I thought. But he knew all right. The slopes above were still dangerous, too steep for him to land the helicopter. He took the body as if it wasn't somebody, just a body, and left.

On that day, Dave and I witnessed the tragic side of mountain-climbing. We never discussed what we had seen, but it gave us glue, a trust, a dark secret. I'd been thinking lately that if I ever went back to exploring, trying desperate, remote routes in the mountains again, Dave would be the right man to go with. When we reached the mountain, if I didn't have the nerve any more, or the desire, he'd understand. I stared out of the train window. Dave would like Patagonia, I thought.

As we pulled into the station, I saw my clients looking up at the west face of the Dru, their faces a strange mixture of terror and awe, fear and desire. It was funny how some mountains made you feel inside.

3

The Wind that Carries Men

Crouching, our hands outstretched, we staggered away from the aircraft, trying to stay on our feet. Inside the small terminal building at Rio Gallegos airport, the other passengers collected their luggage and vanished. We waited for a bus to El Calafate, a small town 350 kilometres to the north. Outside the wind howled, heaving at the heavy steel and glass door of the waiting room. Dave gave me a look, his head cocked to one side, his eyebrows raised.

'Welcome to Patagonia,' he laughed.

'I thought it was supposed to be summer down here.'

'This is ridiculous. How much worse can it get?'

Locals refer to the wind as scouring the land like *la escoba de Dios* – the broom of God. Perhaps it was a warning.

The driver of the empty bus grabbed one of our bags, but on feeling the weight left us to manhandle everything into the luggage compartment ourselves. Jet-lagged, slouched in reclining seats, we stared out over the desolate, windswept landscape somewhere between the mountains and the sea. Borges had understood when he told Theroux, 'You will find nothing there. There is nothing in Patagonia.'

Rio Gallegos itself came to prominence as a port because of the expanding wool trade. There was grass, I suppose, acre upon acre of bleached, stringy-looking grass. During the mid-nineteenth century, eager to claim sovereignty over southern Patagonia, the Argentine government established a naval base and encouraged settlers from Europe, the Falkland Islands and northern Argentina to come and farm. Initially, the native Indians travelled here two or three times a year to coincide with the visits of the steamer boats from Punta Arenas, exchanging guanaco mantles and ostrich feathers for provisions and implements. But the white population grew, claiming more and more land, and introducing disease and alcohol to the Indian tribes. By the middle of the twentieth century, the Indians, their language and culture, so revered by many early travellers, were virtually extinct.

During the latter half of the nineteenth century, the Salesian Society, founded by St John Bosco in Turin, began expanding rapidly. Mission houses were opened throughout Europe, including one in Battersea, in London, as well as in South America. The 23-year-old Agostini was stationed in Tierra del Fuego and, having been raised in the foothills of the Alps, was well equipped to explore the mountains there and further north in Patagonia.

Agostini was a great sympathiser with the indigenous Indians, who were suffering terribly from the advancing white culture, and his writing is considered the best surviving record of that era. A man of charity, he felt compelled to find a way of integrating Indians into white culture, but he also felt obliged to remain faithful to the miners and farmers who had come to carve out a living from the land. He openly criticised some of the more extreme people he encountered, such as the governor Manuel Señoret, who removed whole tribes under the guise of aiding them, giving them food and clothes whilst actually contributing to the extermination process. Indians were an obstacle to the white man's future plans. Agostini records that many evicted Indians ended up being sold as slaves on the streets of Punta Arenas; countless others were murdered on their land. An English farmer, Sam Hyslop, boasted of using straps and belts made from the skin of dead Indians. McLennan, the notorious Scot, claimed that some days he had killed as many Indians as he had drunk glasses of whisky, and, Agostini notes, he was always drunk.

The sun sank in the sky as the bus sliced northwards, the land lined by fences. Historians claim that America was the last continent to be inhabited, the very tip of South America only being reached and occupied by 10,000 BC. It didn't surprise me.

Thousands of Welsh people emigrated here during the middle of the nineteenth century, abandoning family, friends and a beautiful land. What moved them to do so? Back home, in the cities, their livelihood was precarious and insecure, whilst in more rural areas oppressive landlords made tenants' and workers' lives insupportable. In both cases people felt isolated, socially, religiously and linguistically, unable to express their Welsh identity publicly. Today, 140 years later, language teachers from Wales regularly travel to Patagonia to keep the Welsh language alive amongst Patagonians of Welsh descent.

This land is thick with history, myth and legend. From the English traveller Lady Florence Dixie to George Chaworth Musters, from Paul Theroux to Bruce Chatwin, Patagonia is a place in the mind as much as anything, another country, somewhere to lose your old self and begin anew. Wasn't that why I was here?

Dave and I left the bus in El Calafate and met an enthusiastic man standing in the dark, boasting about his guest house, while shielding us from other hoteliers.

'*Es muy bueno, y barato tambien.*'

Totally exhausted, I could have slept right there in the road. We went with him in a taxi.

The next morning we walked along the main street, our eyes squinting as the wind ripped along the ground, blasting our cheeks with dust.

'Remind me to put my ski goggles on next time,' Dave laughed, his eyes still closed.

It took most of the day to shop for food and it forced me to use the modest Castilian I had picked up living in Bilbao.

In the afternoon, the wind still blew hard, and I felt sorry for a couple of men trying to work up on one of the many corrugated-steel roofs. The owner of the guest house arranged spaces for us on the bus to El Chaltén the following day. From there we hoped to hire horses to help us carry the equipment up to a camp beneath our mountain, Fitzroy. Shattered after packing all our food and equipment, we went in search of dinner.

'I want what they're having,' said Dave, his nose against the glass.

Inside, a pyramid of lamb sat between two men, an impressive roast for any large dinner party.

'That is exactly what I want,' Dave said. 'To start with anyhow.'

It had been a long day and I felt hungry too, but even so the portions were absurd.

'Looks about right,' said Dave with a laconic grin when the waiter brought out the meat.

On the mountain I knew that we wouldn't be eating anything quite like this, and with the aid of a bottle of decent red wine, I managed two chunks of lamb and gave the third to Dave. Outside, we walked along the strip in the dark, digesting the food, gazing at the stars, excited about seeing the mountains properly the following day.

'A nightcap?'

We turned back towards the guest house and found a small bar, rapid Spanish flying out of a TV in the corner. A man sat behind the counter.

'*Dos cervezas, por favor usted.*'

A few minutes later a woman came in and sat on a stool with her back towards us, smoking. She was the only other person in there. Until very recently Calafate had been a small, remote sheep-grazing town. Twenty years ago, climbers wanting to reach El Chaltén cheaply had to get a lift with the postman, who passed through just once a fortnight. But encouraged by the government, visits by tourists to the neighbouring Glacier National Park and El Chaltén were increasing. The town seemed dead, though: perhaps more visitors would arrive in a few weeks, nearer Christmas.

Our luggage had expanded so much that the following morning we had to make two trips in a taxi to the bus station. We waited. The minutes ticked by.

'*Usted hay un autobus par el Calafate aqui?*' I asked a man.

'*Aqui no hay,*' he said. 'Maybe in the other street.' He pointed towards the supermarket.

We grabbed our heavy packs and set off running. A small white bus waited on the corner.

'Get on and sit down. We're late.' The driver sounded annoyed.

'We've got more luggage, at the bus station,' I pleaded.

'I have to leave.'

'But what about our bags?'

'Another bus will bring them, don't worry.'

'But . . .'

'I'm sorry, we need to go,' he said, and pulled away.

Tired, hot and embarrassed at having held up the other passengers, we sat down.

How would I explain this to the Mount Everest Foundation Committee, who'd given us considerable financial support? I had to write a report on our return, a document that would be stored in the libraries of the Alpine Club and the Royal Geographical Society for posterity and the benefit of future explorers. 'Dear Sir, The West Face of Fitzroy Expedition (1998) members decided to run away from all their food supplies in order to catch a bus.' That didn't sound right. 'Dear Committee, Due to unforeseen circumstances, $500 worth of food was lost in the bus station.' It was too implausible, whichever way I presented it. Not so much an heroic epic as sheer incompetence; more Rum Doodle than Shackleton. There was nothing for it, I would just have to lie. 'Whilst approaching base camp one of the horses slipped and fell 1000 feet into a steep ravine! The food was never seen again. The expedition was called off immediately.' Was that too extreme?

'If it's gone, it's bad, very bad. We can't afford to buy all that again,' commented Dave, staring directly ahead. He'd put on his sunglasses.

My spirits lifted a little as we glimpsed the faint outline of mountains ahead, beyond the enormous, dazzling Lago Argentina. Fully loaded, the minibus moved slowly, and when other vehicles occasionally passed we disappeared into a cloud of dust, the stuff fighting its way into the bus, powdering everyone's faces. Some people wore scarves over their mouths, others sank behind shirt collars or hands; a couple coughed and sneezed.

As a traveller you are generally a stranger, with little connection to the landscape, its history, its myths, ignorant of previous travellers' exploits. Not all visitors leave a record of their adventures. The pioneering German aviator Gunther Plüschow, however, kept a diary. He was tragically killed here in 1931 when his float plane, the *Silberkondor*, disappeared into the Lago Argentina.

During the 1920s and 1930s, planes were primarily used for war, entertainment, setting records and carrying mail. Plüschow started out as a German navy pilot. He was stationed in northern China, and in 1914 crash-landed during an intelligence-gathering mission, eventually making his way to America and then back to Europe before being arrested in Gibraltar. He was taken as a prisoner of war to Donington Hall, in the Midlands, but escaped and got back to Germany, the only POW to do so during the First World War.

As a young man Plüschow had seen a photograph of a steamer boat moored off the coast of Tierra del Fuego and it had captured his imagination. In 1927 he set sail on his boat, the *Feuerland*, and with his plane, a BMW-powered Heinkel HD-24, made groundbreaking flights across Tierra del Fuego and Patagonia, filming along the way. Ultimately, he had to sell the boat to fund a trip to Germany to try and refinance his expedition. In 1931 he returned to South America to continue exploring. During a normal approach to land at Lago Argentina, witnesses saw the plane invert. The cameraman, Ernest Dreblow, fell first, clutching a parachute. Plüschow followed wearing his parachute, but sadly it caught on the rear of the plane and he was dragged into the shallow lake to his death. Dreblow died from hypothermia a few hours later. Miraculously, Plüschow's diary was recovered.

In 1937, another chronicler of Patagonia, Agostini, teamed up with Franco Bianco, a record-breaking pilot of Piedemont descent who was based in Punta Arenas. His plane, *Saturno*, was a Hawk Major, built in Reading and shipped to Patagonia in 1935. Agostini wrote that he didn't worry about wearing a parachute: 'Two Chilean policemen guard the plane. When I climb into the cockpit, one of them asks me why I don't put on the parachute. I think to myself that the only parachute I always carry with me is a relic of St Juan Bosco, who I invoke in times of difficulty and danger.'

During a four-hour flight over the Torres del Paine and Fitzroy group, Agostini took a series of breathtaking photos, the ones in his magnificent book that had inspired me to come here in the first place.

'Are you going to do some trekking?' I asked the man next to me.

'Yes, we hope so. And you?'

'Well . . . we're climbers, we want to climb some of the peaks here.' Why did I always feel awkward saying that we were climbers? Probably uncomfortable with sounding in any way superior.

'Like Fitzroy, maybe?' The man smiled as if to call my bluff.

'Yes, Fitzroy, if the weather permits.'

'Really? You must be very experienced. And you are alone, only two people?'

I saw Dave turn away and look through the window. He hated the limelight; not unduly shy, but an extremely modest man.

'We climb a lot together, it's what we do, I guess.' I felt myself cringe. 'And you?'

'Oh, we want to do some trekking in the Fitzroy area, then maybe to Torres del Paine.'

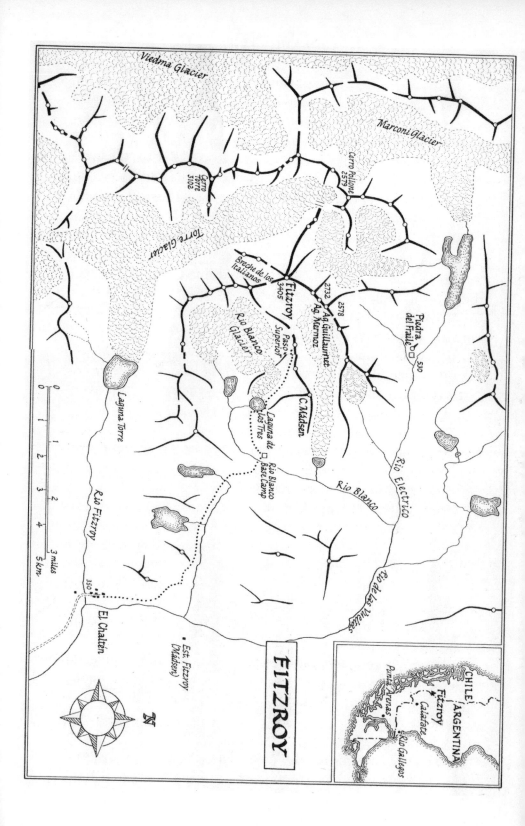

'That will be nice,' I said, lying, knowing that as a climber, walking around the base of the peaks simply staring at them would be torturous. Elaine often joked that I would only walk if the promise of a climb waited at the end of it. The idea of a walk for its own sake was anathema to me. But on this trip I was unsure how I was going to react when standing below the climb, whether or not I still had the courage for it. I needed to find out.

Suddenly the bus began sliding. The driver battled to straighten the vehicle until at last it stopped and we spilled outside. The driver cursed and then spoke into the dusty mouth-piece of his radio, explaining that we had a puncture and would be arriving late. I stared at the pampas turning gold in the sun, and wondered how you would survive alone in a place like this.

Ahead, the mountains fired arrow-like clouds into the blank blue sky. Among the grass, beyond the fence of an isolated estancia, tiny yellow flowers trembled in the wind, miniature jewels in the nothingness. The land revealing itself a little.

When the bus finally reached the Rancho Grande Hostel, the mountains had disappeared into a cool black night. We had planned to economise and camp, but feeling the warmth leaking out through the hostel door, we weakened.

'There will be plenty of opportunities for suffering up there,' I said, pointing towards the sky.

The following morning we watched clouds streaming from the summit of Fitzroy.

'Reasonably impressive,' said Dave, tongue in cheek.

I raised the binoculars and scanned the vast, ice-streaked wall. It was so complex I didn't know where to focus. I felt weak and energised simultaneously. I handed the binoculars over. Words seemed inadequate, empty vessels. You might photograph this mountain half decently, but the feeling was essentially ephemeral, existing fully but only in the moment, and deeply personal.

Agostini had explored this area on foot prior to flying over it with Bianco, and the mountain had clearly inspired him:

'He is the lord of all this vast mountainous region,' he wrote. 'Fitzroy is without a doubt one of the most beautiful and imposing mountains of the Patagonian range.'

The first recorded white man to see the mountain was the Spaniard Antonio de Viedma in 1782. Back then it had the local Indian name Chaltén – 'the mountain that smokes' in the Tehuelche tongue. The frequent cloud around its summit reminded the Indians of the volcanoes they had seen. The Argentinian geographer Francisco Moreno, who did much to promote the population of Patagonia, decided to name it Fitzroy in honour of the captain of the *Beagle*; Robert Fitzroy and Charles Darwin had come relatively close to the area by sailing up the Santa Cruz river in three whaling boats 50 years earlier. Like Chomolungma becoming Everest, perhaps it was an attempt to push forward the boundary of empire and legitimise it; like stealing a beautiful necklace and filing off the previous owner's name.

Moreno had been sent to the area to try and settle a border dispute with neighbouring Chile; an issue still unresolved today. As we turned our backs on the mountain and headed for breakfast, a giant lorry arrived loaded high with building materials. Behind the hostel at least three new buildings were under construction. The Argentine government was zealously handing out land free of cost in an attempt to increase Chaltén's population and turn it into a significant border town.

'That face is one and a half kilometres high.'

'Don't remind me,' I said, reaching for the coffee.

'The Freney Pillar on Mont Blanc is only five hundred metres and El Capitan is only a thousand, isn't it?'

'More or less. And it doesn't have ice stuck all over it – or at least it didn't when I climbed it.'

'It probably didn't have hurricane winds either.'

'No, this ain't California.'

'Ah well, I know you like a challenge, Andy.'

'You know, for once in my life I fancy going trekking.'

Dave laughed. 'I'll quote you on that. You're getting soft in your old age.'

After breakfast, we pored over Andy Parkin's sketches and scribblings, a dog-eared Patagonia treasure map.

'What's that say there?'

'Is it a bivvy spot on the glacier?'

'No, lower down, look: "pans under Alberto's shed".'

'He did mention he had a stash of stuff here in a bag somewhere. Might be useful if our stuff doesn't show up.'

Andy Parkin's map also pointed out new route potential as well as short cuts across glaciers and advice on where to dig snow holes. We took this as a display of his trust in us. He didn't always offer such generosity, but perhaps the vast potential here meant he could relax his normal caginess. Andy held an extreme view towards alpinism and exploration generally, perhaps one of the purist exponents of the game I had ever met. He openly questioned authorities or organisations that made access to the mountains too easy, arguing that individuals should use imagination to travel in wild places and take responsibility for their actions. I glanced at his treasure map again, wondering what he had left out.

Late that afternoon we heard that our food had been found: it would be here tomorrow. Earlier we had found the shed guarding caches of climbers' equipment, bags daubed with 'Donini', 'Silvaterra' and 'Parkin', a sort of who's who of elite Patagonian climbers. We had met a French couple, Bruno Sourzac and his girlfriend Laurence Monnieur, two other Patagonian aficionados. They had endured over a month of appalling weather without reaching any summits. Guides from Chamonix, they had made numerous very impressive ascents the previous year. The issue, they explained, was that the prevailing weather comes from the west, which means that if you climb on a west face, as we had planned, you see the weather approaching but receive the full brunt of it. The flip side is that on an east face you are more sheltered from the wind, but you don't appreciate the scale of a storm until it's too late. A great choice, I thought, given the perpetual storms.

In the end we agreed to try the east side of Fitzroy, as we were both terrible at sitting around in bad weather. And I hoped that the sooner I got some climbing under my belt, the sooner I would relax.

'More sheltered this side!' read Parkin's scribble next to a jagged kiddie's mountain drawn on the far right of his treasure map. He had shown me photos of this steep 500-metre east face of Guillamet. Lots of new thin ice climbs to do, he'd claimed. Fine, as long as you had a good imagination.

The morning we left El Chaltén, a huge cloud trailed from the summit of Fitzroy, a tapering curtain of grey silk. Gaucho Don Guerra's leathered hands tightened ropes, securing the first of our bags to a horse. Guerra had moved here from San Martin de Londres in the north during the 1980s, and he had found a wonderful spot. Nestled below this forested hillside, his small house was protected from the prevailing wind.

We paid Guerra's wife for the eggs and the 12 fresh loaves of bread she'd baked for us as Guerra prepared the horses. Calm and methodical, he had a confident demeanour, an almost melancholic look that could be mistaken for arrogance.

'We wait for you?' I asked.

From behind the horse, both hands occupied, he shook his head and then nodded towards the mountain, encouraging us to set off. On the Tibetan plateau I had seen the nomadic yak herders steal from westerners. They were big people who carried knives and it was difficult to argue. Guerra carried a huge knife too, but we didn't worry. In a small place like this, a negative reputation would destroy his business in no time; besides, being reunited with our food meant we trusted everyone we met. We set off walking towards Rio Blanco, up through a small wooden gate and into the forest.

Soon Dave pulled ahead and I wandered alone along the small worn path. We had begun the journey proper now, no more buses, planes or trains; feet only. Mosses hung in the trees and unfamiliar birds crisscrossed above, calling tunes alien to my ears. When the path emerged from the forest, the land changed dramatically. Trees torn and ravaged by the wind were strewn along a sand bank; strange, more animated and more alive than the green breathing forest I'd just left. Fat sleeping silver trunks, discarded, half buried. Thinner trunks, their branches like the naked limbs of dead soldiers, lay frozen in impossible positions, gesticulating at the sky. I put my pack down and rested, remembering how much I loved the wild.

As the river ran by, I glanced up at the towering satellite summits either side of Fitzroy, reminders of previous bold adventurers. Straight across sat Poincenot, a tremendous needle of vertical rock with a hanging glacier glued to its right side. On the expedition that made the first ascent of Fitzroy in 1952 (before many of the bridges were built), Jacques Poincenot had been crossing a river attached to a fixed safety rope. He slipped, became trapped underwater in a strong current and was unable to unclip himself from the rope. He drowned. On reaching the summit, Don Whillans hammered a French piton into the rock as a mark of respect for Poincenot. Whillans' partner, Frank Cochrane, dropped an Argentinian coin into a crack.

Further left, lower but mightily impressive, sat Saint-Exupéry, named by Agostini in honour of the French pioneering mail pilot here in Patagonia during the late 1920s. To the right of Fitzroy stood two steep peaks, Mermoz and Guillamet, once again named by Agostini after heroic French pilots, colleagues of Saint-Exupéry. The trio had worked as commercial pilots in South America, which, like Alaska, had a burgeoning mail industry at that time. Saint-Exupéry was appointed as operations manager for the newly opened Patagonian route. The heroic adventures of flying through fierce windstorms and over hostile, barren land were short lived, as the employer, Aeropostale, went bankrupt. His tales, recounted in literary Paris cafés, provided the material for his remarkable book *Night Flight* (1931).

Unlike mountaineering, which has a long-established literary tradition, stories of pioneering pilots are relatively scarce. This is probably because aviation moved from pioneering (1900–1930s) to commercial passenger air travel (1950s) relatively quickly.

The writing that does exist tends to be romantic and nostalgic, as if mourning the loss of those more adventurous times when inside smaller aircraft you were aware of the ground beneath you.

Saint-Exupéry himself disappeared in 1944 during a military mission off the south coast of France. In 1998 a fisherman found a bracelet belonging to him off the island of Riou near Marseille. Two years later a diver discovered a crashed Lockheed P-38 Lightning, which French experts confirmed was Saint-Exupéry's plane.

I could get used to this life, I told myself as I moved on, meeting Dave sitting by a small bridge that spanned a river fuelled by meltwater from the glacier at the base of Fitzroy. We climbed uphill, crossed another river and met Gaucho Don Guerra on the edge of the forest, unsaddling our equipment from the horses. Using his local knowledge of small trails, he had somehow overtaken us.

'How much do we owe you, Don Guerra?' I asked once he'd finished.

'*Bueno*, twenty-five dollars for each horse and thirty-five for me.'

I handed him the money.

'And the rope, maybe we will leave you the rope once we have finished on the mountain.'

'Sure, I can always use rope,' he said, pointing at the horses and at their tackle, made from climbing rope left by past expeditions.

Not for the first time, I wondered what had brought Guerra and his type to this land. Historically, the motivation to uproot and move to Patagonia had been a necessity, as in the case of James Radbourne of Berkshire, soon to be known as 'El Jimmy'. Most new arrivals were greeted with the question: 'Was it a girl or poaching?' In Jimmy's case, it was both.

When he arrived, the gold rush was at its peak, and Punta Arenas, being a stopping-off point for miners, had all the expected trappings: gambling, violence and plenty of brothels.

Jimmy and his sort roamed around, often working for absent farm-owners who simply wanted returns. He loved the freedom of the life, but various skirmishes earned him a reputation as a hard man. He moved north, was convicted of a crime he didn't commit, but managed to escape from prison. He now began living as an outlaw in the rugged Andean foothills, where it was easier to forget a culprit than pursue him. Jimmy took refuge from the law with the native Tehuelche Indians, living in *toldos*, guanaco-skin tents. He grew to respect them and under their guidance became an expert horseman, learning how to hunt from a galloping horse using bolas, stones encased in leather and roped together.

Before long, Jimmy fell in love with an Indian girl named Juana, the niece of Mulato, one of the most powerful Patagonian Indian chiefs. During a horse race for her hand in marriage, one of his enemies, Montenegro, swindled Jimmy and left with Juana. Years later, Montenegro was jailed, and Jimmy finally joined up with Juana, with whom he had four children. In his later years, Jimmy claimed the rights to his own land and became semi-respectable. He could still shock visitors, though, describing such things as the popular Indian pick-me-up for a hangover: a mixture of the raw kidney, liver, heart and blood of a guanaco. His other favourite anecdote described a gaucho who bit off an Italian's ear during a fight and then forced him to swallow it.

The gauchos still had a reputation as strong, independent men who lived on the fringes of society.

We shook Don Guerra's hand. It was a lifeless, un-enthusiastic shake. Some people said it was like that with the gauchos in the beginning. They had no reason to trust you; it would become firmer after a few meetings. With little cere-mony he gave us a gentle wave, then quietly turned and headed back to Chaltén. We were in the mountains proper now; this was our country.

Next to a water trough carved from wood, a sign had been nailed to a stake in the ground. 'RIO BLANCO CLIMBERS ONLY' read the yellow letters. Our bags were by a perfect place for camping just inside the forest, under a canopy of beech trees, one of which had a hole where a woodpecker flew in.

'This is my kind of base camp,' I smiled.

The wind had fallen and we wore only T-shirts. We had endured some grim base camps over the years, especially in northern Pakistan, in the Karakorum. There, tents were often pitched on ice at heights well above 5000 metres, and the only available water came from the glacier full of silt. There would be no altitude problems here, and the water turned out to be pristine. It reminded me of an alpine meadow in late spring. I imagined the land had probably remained unchanged over the years, but I was mistaken. The 1952 French Fitzroy team had met and chatted frequently with the Dane Andreas Madsen, the first permanent white settler in this area.

'The pioneers were not destructive,' he told them. '[But] the companies: their behaviour was disastrous. When their gangs arrived to cut wood for building and poles for fencing, they weren't content with cutting only what they required, they burned the rest. In the same way they killed the deer simply for the pleasure of killing. They massacred dozens at a time, trying out their guns, and they left the bodies to rot... I protested to the government asking that they should keep some part of the land as a nature reserve for the deer and foxes. But it was in vain.'

Madsen had a friendly relationship with the Tehuelche Indians. 'When I was poor and alone they gave me generous and disinterested help ... Not so long ago they were the sole lords of Patagonia. Now there are very few of them left. One more generation and they will have disappeared altogether through inter-marriage with other races, tuberculosis, and the abuse of alcohol. They are a dying race but I shall always treasure the memory of those fat kindly silent men ... If I were the last man left to protest I should remain opposed to progress and saddened by the destruction of nature and local traditions.'

Deeper in the woods at the Rio Blanco site were a group

of six carefree Argentinian climbers. Following an attempt at Fitzroy earlier in the year, when they had left some fixed ropes in place, they had returned, travelling overland from their home town of Buenos Aires. Some were busy cooking, one of them played a guitar, another whittled a piece of wood.

'*Y ustedes?* Where are you climbing?'

'We wanted to climb on the west face, but with these winds, we thought we would try this side,' I said. 'Maybe we'll go to the west face when the weather improves.'

The alarm sounded at 3 a.m., a faint beep almost lost in the groaning of the trees that swayed like the masts of tall ships riding a huge swell. Dave reset the alarm and we drifted off back into sleep until 6 a.m., when the wind was if anything even stronger.

Dave opened the tent door. 'I can't believe it, a team of trekkers are going up.'

After porridge and tea, we helped each other into the shoulder straps of the heavy rucksacks. We found a decent path and it felt good to be moving, though walking in my big mountain boots felt clumsy. I hadn't worn them since Changabang, almost two years ago now. The wind increased as we gained height, and when we reached the upper lake, we found it difficult to stand. The wind froze my fingers and thighs. I dropped my pack to the ground and began pulling on more clothes. Terrified of losing my gloves, I placed large stones on them until I'd zipped up my pants and jacket.

There may have been a case for returning to the woods immediately, save for the fact that the three trekkers were up ahead of us. The gale beat down the white slope, sweeping snow across the frozen lake to where the trekkers swayed. They were taking photos of each other, leaning at ludicrous angles, supported by the force of the wind. They had reached their intended highpoint now and set off back down. Struggling to see in the searing wind, we stopped again and put on our goggles. The base of Fitzroy revealed itself, grey and orange walls disappearing into the cloud, a suggestion of what lay

ahead. Full of purpose, keen to prove my worth as a mountaineer, to myself and to the trekkers, I stumbled forward.

'The snow slope above the lake on the right looks like wind
slab. Left looks better.'

'You what?' Dave screamed, trying to compete with the
hurricane winds.

I lifted my gloved hand and stabbed the air to my left. 'Better
on the left, safer,' I bellowed, and we marched on.

At a small frozen stream we came to a stop. On the left,
the stream dropped away dramatically and a strong updraught
blew water back up, coating the rocks in thin clear ice. I concentrated, using my ski pole for balance, invigorated by all the
excitement, attempting to step only on rocks clear of ice. Small
drops of water spray hit the edge of my goggles and froze.
This is absurd, I thought. Without the wind I would be happy
taking a dog for a walk up here. As it is, we may not make it
to the base of the snow slope on the other side of the lake.
Though safe from avalanche, this route around the lake involved
negotiating a rocky outcrop. It didn't look as if we'd need a
rope, though. I set off, skirting the cliff until level with a shelf
that ran horizontally rightwards, 40 feet above the lake. Halfway
across, the shelf became uncomfortably narrow and I couldn't
fathom where to go.

'Down,' Dave shouted.

I nodded. A ramp slanted towards the lake; the thin cracks
in its black frozen skin had filled with loose white snow like
the seams in a patchwork quilt. I was moving slowly, unnerved
by the exposure, when suddenly a fist of wind smacked me in
the ribs. I swayed, my boots slipping sideways along the small
granite footholds. I gripped tight with my hands and felt fear
flush my cheeks. I stared at the lake and imagined what would
happen if I fell and plunged through the ice. Fastened to a
pack this size, I would sink fast. If I undid the chest harness
and waist belt, I might have a chance of swimming out. But
the unpredictable gusts of wind meant that was suicidal. It was
a cold wind, but now I sweated as I set off down the ramp.
Not far to go. Suddenly a rock hit my forehead. Blood filled

one of my eyes, and I squinted up trying to see where it had come from. I wiped my face with my glove and carried on towards the flat rock shelf beyond the lake.

'It's not deep, Andy,' yelled Dave, looking at my gash.

A moderate scramble had become all-out combat, and we couldn't envisage making it much further. Dave pointed at a collection of large boulders up ahead. We now felt the power of the wind increase. *Escoba de Dios* was too gentle a term; this was the work of the devil. Abruptly, the wind ripped me from my feet and I shot through the air, landing on my side, unhurt but shocked. I crawled towards Dave, who crouched behind a large rock, shaking his head. We hadn't even reached the edge of the glacier yet. We left a stash of equipment in a sealed bag, buried it under stones and set off back down. Despite 20 years of battling in the Scottish highlands, we had never experienced anything like this before.

4

Freedom and Exile

Just after midday, two new recruits arrived at the Rio Blanco camp: a tall girl with long dark hair named Steph, and Charlie, an older, thick-set man who wore dark sunglasses. The noise of the wind from our disastrous attempt to reach the base of the mountain still rang in my ears, and after shaking Charlie's firm hand, I decided to talk him through the current weather patterns and point out the absolute futility of leaving the forest. Unfortunately, I was too slow.

'Do you know what, guys?' Charlie began, staring up towards Fitzroy. 'If I was up on the mountain today, I'd be loving it, yeah.'

Dave and I froze, jaws lowered.

'I'm tellin' you, I'd have a T-shirt on, shades, just beautiful, mighty fine day for a real long route up high, what you reckon, Steph?'

'Sounds good, Charlie.'

I wanted to mention the fact that I'd been picked up by the wind and dumped on the ground, wanted to show him the cut on my head, but I didn't.

'It seemed really windy to us,' I said instead, rather pathetically.

'Windy, oh boy, this ain't windy.'

I hid in the tent for the remainder of the afternoon.

'Andy, do you know who that is?'

'No.'

'I'm sure it's Charlie Fowler. The lass is Steph Davis, I've seen her in the mags – an amazing crack climber, apparently.'

I rarely read climbing magazines any more, but I'd heard of Charlie. For years he had climbed audacious new routes all over the globe, including in the Himalayas and even on far-flung Scottish sea cliffs. He was something of a legend down here in Patagonia.

'Maybe I should just admit I'm not cut out for this any more. It seemed pretty bloody windy to me up there.'

'Andy, it was madly windy, even by Scottish standards.'

'By anybody's standards,' I barked.

The reason the area gets battered by ruthless winds is simple enough. The Fitzroy massif more or less sits at a latitude of 50 degrees, the infamous 'furious fifties' (further south and more powerful than the 'roaring forties'). The west wind races in from the Pacific Ocean unhindered, charging across the Patagonian ice cap until it smashes into the first thing that blocks its path; these 10,000-foot towers of rock and ice. With power to spare, it then rampages eastward across the steppe. The wind played with us, like a giant hairdryer blowing ants from the side of a pepper pot.

The weather and conditions in Patagonia certainly left an impression on legendary climbers Lionel Terray and Guido Magnone, who succeeded in making the first ascent of Fitzroy in 1952. The climbing itself had been relentless and Terray began worrying about the consequences of getting trapped high on the mountain. 'I lost the courage and wanted to turn back while there was still time, but Magnone's iron resolve won me over.' The remoteness, incessant bad weather and verglas-plastered rocks prompted Terray to write afterwards: 'Of all the climbs I have done, the Fitzroy was the one on which I most nearly approached my physical and moral limits.' Making a fast free ascent of the Terray line on Fitzroy was something Dave and I were considering.

Ignoring our instincts, spying the Americans at the other

side of the camp packing their rucksacks for an early morning departure spurred us into action. If anything the wind appeared worse than on our previous attempt, but we were determined to get a little higher. By the first hint of sunrise we had reached our cache of equipment beyond the lake. We leaned into the wind comically, our heels lifting off the ground, our faces hidden beneath goggles and balaclavas, gesticulating with gloved hands like a pair of astronauts. It wasn't so steep but we used two ice axes to guard against the frequent, unexpected punch of the wind. A few hundred metres above the lake, I turned around and snapped a photo of Dave. Ridge upon ridge of gold-tinted peaks faded to the east and spectacular white cigar clouds raced above. In the bottom left corner of the swaying viewfinder I saw two small dots turn around and, with the help of the wind, race back towards the forest; it was Steph and Charlie.

On the spur leading up to the Passo Superior, the wind eased a little, but at the pass itself, it found its strength again. Shards of ice flew through a blue sky overhead and an extraordinary noise filled the air, as if we were sitting in the path of a jumbo jet coming in to land. Dave lunged repeatedly at the bank of wet snow with his ice axe shaft, eventually finding the entrance to an existing snow hole. Digging, improving the tunnel into the chamber, kept you warm, but with only enough room for one, we alternated so that the other didn't freeze. Our clothes were soaked. In the Boy Scouts I remembered studying pictures of snow holes in a book with excitement; I never imagined as a young boy that I'd end up being imprisoned in one for almost a month.

We crouched shoulder to shoulder, miserable, cramped, wondering how we'd manage to sleep. Water dripped from the roof. When Dave suggested that we expand the hole before getting our sleeping bags out, I commented that I understood smaller caves to be warmer. Dave gave me a searching look, the engineer in him silently questioning the theory. I held to my spurious fact and, perhaps believing I had picked up the tip during my mountain guides' exam, he complied. The reality was that I felt exhausted and had no energy for home improvements right then; I needed food and sleep. We started the stove and shuffled into our sleeping bags, the moisture produced by the pan of melting snow joining forces with the increased drips from the roof of the cave.

'This cave was obviously used by someone else,' I started.

'Yes, a group of mountaineering midgets,' Dave snapped, and then added, 'who enjoyed sitting in puddles.'

I began to regret the theory of small snow caves, but despite the misery, we managed to sleep.

The following morning, we were struck by the absolute silence. Perhaps the weather had finally changed; the storm had run out of breath. Not a chance. We wriggled and dug our way out of the hole to find that almost a metre of new snow had fallen and was continuing to fall, the wind flinging flakes into the beams of our lights. We retreated into the icy coffin and tried to doze. A German climber, Karl Reinhard, once remarked that mountaineering in Patagonia was akin to sitting in an electrical deep freezer setting fire to hundred-dollar bills. I calculated we'd already burned three or four thousand dollars and we hadn't even reached the base of the mountain. When it became light, we set off down.

As we entered the camp, we met Charlie.

'Gee, guys, that was one hell of a breeze up there.'

We took it as a compliment.

'I never thought I would experience winds worse than Scotland,' I began, 'but this place takes first prize.'

'You bet,' said Charlie, every line in his face hinting at a story. From what I understood, he was an American equivalent of Andy Parkin, someone who had sacrificed and suffered for the pure alpine ethic; relaxed, but with a voracious appetite for the game.

Through the afternoon I enjoyed lounging in the tent, reading, staring out at the forest, trying to spot the woodpecker. Unexpectedly, Steph approached. Her milk-white teeth and luxuriant jet-black hair were slightly out of place in this camp.

Her arrival had sent all of us into a frenzied search for razors and combs.

'Hi, Steph,' I called as she strolled over.

'Hi, Andy. I'd really like to show you my puppy.'

This took me by surprise. Where I come from, this is code for *voulez-vous coucher avec moi*, or, to be more precise, would you like to have rampant sex. Dave was off scrubbing the pans. Charlie was God knows where. I felt quite helpless as she entered the tent.

'He's called Fletcher.'

'You what?'

She put her hand into her jacket.

'Look, this is my puppy, Fletcher. Isn't he sweet?' She held out a photograph of a small brown-and-white dog.

'He looks great,' I said.

'I miss him so much.'

'I'm sure he misses you too.'

'You guys should come over to our cabin for coffee sometime.'

'Thanks.'

Three ramshackle wooden cabins had been built by climbers over the years at the Rio Blanco camp. Charlie and Steph had taken the middle cabin. On our return, we had begun using the one nearest the stream, for no other reason than we had it to ourselves. Or so we thought. That evening, whilst eating supper by the light of my head torch, I saw countless pairs of eyes emerge from the wooden walls. The decision to come to Patagonia had been mainly because of the luxuriant campsites, lack of altitude and short distances to the base of the peaks. So far we had yet to see the peaks at close range and our camps currently oscillated between an annoyingly wet miniature snow cave and a dark, rat-infested shed.

After supper, Dave placed a small paper bag on the cabin floor with half a biscuit inside and then stood over it with a long, heavy club of wood, waiting. His frustration at the miserable weather had been transformed into malevolent concentration. Within a couple of minutes, the first rat, or *laucha*, scurried across the floor before tiptoeing into the bag. As swift as a samurai, Dave powered the club down on to the bag, sending a shockwave around the cabin. But the *laucha* had played before and vanished in a flash. One hour later and a packet of biscuits worse off, we gave up. Meanwhile, 30 metres away, unbeknown to us, the Argentinians were employing a gentler, more sophisticated approach with impressive results. They had whittled a long, slim pole of wood of a precise length with sharpened pencil-like edges and balanced it across a deep bowl full of water. Placing food in the middle of the slippery pole enticed the beasts to try their luck. Once committed with both front legs, they lost their grip as the pole spun, fell into the water and drowned.

The air pressure rose during the night, and at 4 a.m. we set off towards the snow cave. By the time we arrived, though, thick wet snow covered our helmets and goggles.

'I thought it sounded like bollocks,' said Dave, as I admitted to my fabricated mini-snow-cave theory.

Bruno and Laurence passed on their descent. They had camped on the edge of the glacier in a tent made of para-chute material, and looked cold; damp beyond the superficial cheer. We migrated into an adjacent, slightly bigger snow hole and set about enlarging it.

We felt ready for a challenge now and longed for a spell of decent weather; one full day without wind would be a start. At midnight Dave got out of his sleeping bag, put on his boots and waterproofs and squirmed through the tunnel to look outside. Snow was still falling in a fresh breeze. At 2 a.m. it was my turn, but nothing had changed. We were putting ourselves through a sleep deprivation torture programme. Each weather check took almost 15 minutes. At 4 a.m., Dave's alarm sounded.

'Wakey, wakey, Andrew,' he said in a silly, excited voice.

We ate a small breakfast and then left. We climbed up on to the glacier that flowed to the foot of Fitzroy and tied on to the rope; alone, silent, our nerves tingling. The pink-grapefruit snow glistened in the first sun as we ploughed a trail up the slope, our lungs stinging in the fresh dawn air. We had dispensed with bivouac equipment and kept our gear to a bare minimum, but still my chest worked overtime trying to keep pace with Dave, who strained ahead, stretching the rope like a husky on the edge of the Arctic. We were both afraid of losing precious time, unsure of how long the weather would stay calm.

Dave set off up the first steep section of our route, chopping and hooking his ice axes, wrestling with an overhanging mass of ice tentacles that oozed from a blank vertical granite wall. I waited, craning my neck around, staring at the unfathomable east face that plunged from the summit to the glacier 1500 metres below, surely one of the most difficult walls in the whole of the Andes.

Suddenly, the place made sense. I witnessed the austere beauty of Patagonia, felt its magic, and with it came a subtle but deep calm. I thought of the priest Agostini and why he had been compelled to enter deep into these mountains, further than others had dared. Perhaps feeling caught between the plight of the Indians and the new white settlers, he came here to the mountains to make sense of things, or perhaps to forget; to find beauty in the hardship of moving up over snow and rock, an activity inexplicable but therapeutic, pointless yet essential.

In the sun we moved quickly up to a ridge of rock, our side warm to the touch, the other streaked with shallow hoar frost, like lines of frozen mink pelts. A piercing breeze startled me as I pulled over the ridge and looked to the west, to Cerro Torre and the ice cap that stretched on beyond. I cowered back to shelter, put on a hat and gloves and set off again. I climbed cautiously, along the icy granite spine; a dark, fathomless gully plunged straight down on my left between two black walls. Concentrating, lost in the movement, any anguish, any uncertainty of how I might feel about mountain-climbing disappeared. It was as if the idea of a big mountain climb, the thought of it, had become a larger obstacle than the mountain itself. Perhaps I had plunged too deeply into thought and forgotten the simple pleasure of action, the poetry from the control of crampons in ice, the grip of fingers around the rope that fell from a friend's waist. The trust. The belief of two people, the power of it, the strange force. I felt it returning now, despite the wind.

We teetered along an elegant ice ridge until we were beneath a smooth vertical shield of rock split by a thin slanting crack. We forced ourselves to eat and drink a little, and then Dave started scratching and kicking at the crack, which was covered in a treacherous layer of thick verglas. Lionel Terray had probably experienced the same awful conditions, but unlike him, we didn't have any fixed rope to leave in place in case a storm arrived.

If the cloud had blown in earlier, I wouldn't have seen what I saw. Above me, Dave chipped away at the ice with an axe, laboriously trying to clean out the crack, orchestrating protection that might arrest his fall in case he slipped. There was too little ice to take the weight of a crampon point or the tip of an ice axe but enough to conceal all the edges from his hands and feet. Thirty minutes, an hour, an hour and a half, two hours. The wind began to gust strongly and I began to lose belief that we could make it to the top and get back down safely in one day. Dave must have felt the same. Then, down in the icy gully a few hundred feet below us, I spotted someone dressed in red. We hadn't seen a soul all day. I looked for a second climber, but saw no one.

'How much rope?'

I turned and looked up. Dave had almost made it to a sloping ledge where he could secure himself.

I glanced at the rope on the floor and guessed at 40 feet.

'OK, watch me closely here,' Dave shouted. 'This rope looks very dubious.'

The fixed rope left by the Argentinians swayed in the wind. Dave had hold of it in his left arm and was preparing to pull up on it to allow him to move back into the final part of the crack. I fed through more rope and then, though I knew I

Chamonix-based artist and alpinist, Andy Parkin, examining his sculptures

Gunther Plüschow (*left*), with companion, next to his plane *Silberkondor*, Tierra del Fuego, *c.* 1930

Padre di Agostini (*left*) and Franco Bianco, beside *Saturno*, Patagonia, 1937

Tehuelche Indians

Looking towards the Fitzroy massif. Note wind damage to forest.

Gaucho Don Guerra, Rio Blanco base camp

Cabin life, Rio Blanco. *Left to right*: Top alpinists, Trym Sæland, Steph Davis and Charlie Fowler.

East face of Fitzroy at dawn

Dave Hesleden breaking trail on the
Poincenot Glacier, Patagonia

Dave Hesleden tackles the
bergschrund of Fitzroy

Team head towards
east face of Fitzroy
as storm approaches

Dave Hesleden, snow cave, Paso Superior

View down east face. Note damage
to Argentinian fixed rope.

Pioneering on
Guillamet's east face

Andy and Dave at
the Paso Superior

The Famhair headwall in winter, Beinn Bhàn, Applecross, Scotland

Leo Houlding, first ascent, Angel of the North, Tyneside, UK

Andy and Leo in Fiat Romeo, Stavanger, Norway

The Shield takes centre stage, Kjerag, Lysefjord, Rogaland, Norway

Andy fights with upper cracks of Hoka Hey,
during the second free ascent

Leo enjoying the adventure,
Alfa badge in place

Leo takes a fag break
during retreat in rain storm

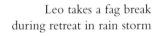

Leo engrossed during the first free ascent of The Shield. Note angle of ropes.

Andy and Leo jubilant on top of Kjerag after freeing The Shield

Britain's Tim Emmet prepares to fly off Kjerag

should have been watching him closely, glanced back down at the gully. Maybe it was an abandoned rucksack, something blown off in the wind or dropped. It was easy to drop a rucksack. I could make out arms, though, both raised up above, clinging to the ice, and it was a steep angle, at least 50 degrees. A bag wouldn't stay on ice that steep. Maybe someone was stuck. From where Dave would finish climbing, you would be able to see more, work out what was happening.

The face hung above oppressively. Isolated chunks of snow protruded from the wall, marble-white busts mounted against the brown-orange rock, remnants of the recent relentless storms. I had become quite cosy perched on the shelf of ice, and when Dave signalled for me to start climbing, I felt a tremendous sense of exposure. A queasiness sat in the pit of my stomach, a negative force, and I started to sweat despite the cold. At the halfway point, I arched my neck back, trying to work out where the route went. Above Dave, streaks of ice coating the rock glinted in the sun like the blades of flashing swords.

'Not ideal,' said Dave when I reached him.

'Well done, Dave, that looked scary.'

'It felt scary. We were moving well until then.' The goggles hid his expression. He pointed to the Argentinians' fixed rope, the innards bursting from the split sheath, frozen and frail.

'What do you reckon? I don't think we'll make it to the top and back down today; I mean, everything's sheathed in ice.'

'I know, and look over there. The summit of Cerro Torre has disappeared into cloud; there's a storm coming in. Let's get the hell out of here.' The wind filled the hood of Dave's jacket as if to underline his words.

'Have you seen that down in the gully? I thought it was someone climbing up.'

'I know. I saw it before.'

We abseiled down on to the ridge and started sorting out the ropes, the wind growing more violent with each passing minute. The light had changed, and when I stared down the gully now, I changed my mind about what it was.

'That's a dead body. Look.'

'I know, mate. I don't want to look.' His voice sounded tender.

'Fucking hell,' I yelled at the wind. 'For fuck's sake.'

'Let's keep moving, mate, that storm looks nasty.'

The thing is, I thought, the thing is . . . and then the wind hit me in the chest. The gust scared me, and I forgot what I was about to think. My eyes filled with water but it was only the wind. It had got into my goggles somehow. Damn wind. Spoilt everything, turned a special day into a bad one, no different to any other day. Dave was right, though, Cerro Torre had gone, smothered by mushrooming cloud. We needed to get down. I cursed under my breath as we retraced our steps carefully and then abseiled all the way to the glacier.

5

Mixed Emotions

'Do you know what, Andy?' said Dave the next day in the snow hole.

'What?'

'You've changed.'

'In what way?'

'It's like you've nothing to prove any more.'

'What do you mean?'

'It doesn't seem so important to you.'

I knew that the experiences of Changabang had changed me, but it was difficult to articulate how in precise terms. Non-climbing friends had asked: 'What is it about going high up? Why do you do it?' And it was hard to answer, because it was about so many things. The urge to climb is natural enough; a small child will expend enormous energy trying to climb up anything that presents itself. As a young boy, I loved to climb trees, buildings or whatever long before I discovered the sport of mountaineering. The mountains provided a natural extension of this, the perfect playground for adulthood.

'I'm still keen, Dave. I love the mountains. They have been my life, but no mountain is worth dying for.'

'I agree, absolutely not.'

'I never want to experience again what happened on Changabang. Never.'

'The problem here is just the weather. You wouldn't want to get trapped high on a route in some of these winds.'

'But you never know how long the weather will stay stable; it could be a few hours, it could be a day.'

'I wonder if this is worse than normal.'

We went outside. It felt pleasantly warm, the wind had died and the sky had cleared. It was a better day than the previous one, but we were exhausted from our Fitzroy attempt. Whilst our ropes, jackets and gloves dried in the sun, we took turns to stare through the binoculars, trying to link up runnels of ice on the east face of Guillamet, one of Fitzroy's smaller neighbours.

'It would be good to do something new.'

'It would be good to do anything,' I replied.

I knew what he meant, though: if you came all this way, it was good to have a proper adventure, and there is no finer adventure than finding your way up a previously unexplored wall.

'You'd need faith,' I said. 'But you might be able to do it in a day.'

'Less chance of getting nailed in a storm.'

'Exactly.'

'Let's have a look tomorrow. We've nothing to lose.'

For some, the lure of Fitzroy was nothing to do with the desire to climb it. For them, it was maybe the raw beauty of the area that drew them, its magic. One such had been Andreas Madsen. Brought up in Jutland, he had a miserable peasant childhood before joining a Baltic ship and arriving in Buenos Aires in the early 1920s aged 20. During a spell working with the group of men trying to delimit the Argentinian frontier, he met an adventurer with whom he travelled to the foot of Fitzroy. This man abandoned him and Madsen endured the winter alone, surviving in a hut made of branches, nursing a broken arm caused by a fall from his horse. Eventually he travelled back to Denmark for his sweetheart, who had waited 14 years, and together they returned to this place and settled. Tragically, his wife died, as did two of their four children. He buried them behind his house beside el Rio de las Vueltas and carved their tombstones himself from the granite of Fitzroy.

The French climbers who met Madsen in 1952 believed he found mountaineering an amusing concept: 'Fitzroy will be climbed one day,' they told him. 'Man never accepts defeat.' Madsen simply shook his head, as if suggesting that it was impossible to break the spell of a mountain even by conquering it.

Unquestionably, Madsen had been motivated by wanderlust, like most who ventured here: how else did you end up living in a place like this? He was also a survivor who had overcome tremendous adversity in his life. But perhaps mountaineering was a luxury he simply didn't have the time or energy for. He had based himself as deep in the mountains as was reasonably possible; no one had ever settled beyond, up on the ice cap. The French climbers, like ourselves, were here only temporarily. Madsen had made his home in the valley below, but he had no urge to explore the mountains in the way Agostini had or as we intended. So what was different?

Pondering this didn't answer the question of my changed relationship with the mountains either.

The sky the following morning superseded anything either of us had ever witnessed in the mountains. Cotton-wool clouds slowly turned through pink, purple and orange, forcing us to stand still, entranced.

'Film's cheap,' said Dave, as he fired off a reel. I tried to catch him in my camera, but I could tell he hated it by the startled look he wore each time I raised the viewfinder to my eye.

I struck the slope with the front of my boots until we were a few feet below a deep fracture line where the glacier broke from the thin tongue of ice that tapered up until vanishing on the vertical horizon.

'I'll lead it,' said Dave confidently.

It looked exactly his forte: thin technical ice with very little protection. He'd established notorious routes of this nature in Scotland and the Alps. Some have never been repeated. I stood aside.

Dave swung his axes one at a time over the fracture line and then threw his left foot up high and stood up. The karabiners and ice screws attached to his harness swung out from his waist, revealing the steepness of the ice. After 20 metres he still hadn't found any solid protection and I turned away, unable to watch. The ice had become so thin that he decided to try and escape into a corner. He swung his foot out on to the wall, frantically trying to find an edge. Once the foot stuck, he swung his axe and transferred his weight across. As he smashed in a piton, he pierced the silence. I knew from the tone that it was bomb-proof. Each blow produced a higher note. I breathed out, a long, slow exhalation, and relaxed. There was nothing I could do to help, but still I found myself tense in such situations, as if I was up there myself.

After three hours Dave reached the sanctuary of a tiny ledge.

'We won't finish it today,' he yelled down. 'We'd have a good chance of making it with an early start, though.'

'What's it look like above?'

'Absolutely amazing. We could leave a rope in place.'

It sounded like a logical plan.

We left as many things as possible in the snow cave and then descended to the forest, meeting the Argentinians coming up. We explained how bad their rope had become up on Fitzroy, which disappointed them, though they had half expected the news. One had a huge piece of wood strapped to the back of his rucksack, two feet long and eight inches wide, perhaps an inch thick.

'What the hell is that?' I asked. It read '*te'amo*', 'I love you' in Spanish.

The others began laughing.

'Oh, it's from my girlfriend. She says I have to take it with me so I don't forget her.' He shrugged his shoulders and smiled. Dave and I had cut the handles off our toothbrushes to save weight, and this guy had a fence post strapped to his back.

'The girls in Buenos Aires must be phenomenal.'

'Some, yes,' he laughed.

We wished them luck and set off with a spring in our step: we had a project now, something to aim for.

At Rio Blanco, Laurence stood by the stream washing clothes. Bruno sat in the sun carving a short piece of knotted wood. They had pitched their tent close to ours and begun sharing the cabin. The French pair looked utterly relaxed, greeting us with big smiles. Bruno disappeared into the cabin and returned with a small mug full of damp green leaves, a silver straw sticking out.

'You want some maté?'

'Sure, I'll try some,' I said. The descent had left my throat dry.

Touched by the gesture, we sat on our rucksacks and waited, watching Bruno organise the beverage, sucking at the pipe and spitting out bits of leaf on to the ground.

He filled the cup with more water and then passed it to me. As soon as the liquid hit my throat I screwed up my face, like a bulldog sucking a bee sting. I turned my head to the side and spat the stuff on the ground.

'I am sorry,' I said. 'It's too bitter for me. Do you have any water, or normal tea?'

Laurence roared with laughter. 'You Englishmen love tea with milk, no?'

'I'm afraid so, a Yorkshire man especially. Let Dave try it.' This was cruel, as I knew he detested anything bitter.

Another round of laughter ensued as Dave began sucking tentatively on the straw before passing it back to Bruno.

'I think we'll leave you to it,' he said.

We were totally ignorant of the significance of *los matés* in Argentine life, whereas Bruno and Laurence had spent months down here in Patagonia. The green stuff is called yerba, a caffeinated herb grown in the more fertile northern provinces. Normally there is one server, or *cerbador* (Bruno). The *cerbador*'s job it is to refill the cup (also known as the maté) with yerba and water for each person, and to clear the metal straw, *la bombilla*. The Indians discovered maté from the Christians and traded animal skins for it. The maté cup is often very ornate, shaped from wood and covered with animal skin stretched thin. It is not uncommon for groups of Argentinians to spend hours enjoying *los matés*, and it seems to be an expression of cultural belonging across generations and classes throughout the country, from judges to gas station attendants. Bruno offering us the drink was a sign of friendship, but we didn't appreciate the gesture and instead made English tea, opened some biscuits and began dunking them into our mugs.

It felt wonderful to be in the forest: the colours of the mosses, the flowers a treat after life in the snow cave. Behind our tent a woodpecker stuck its head out of a small hole observing us, the soft feathers on the rear of its head sticking up like a mohican. Walk just a few minutes away from the camp in almost any direction and the forest seemed totally unspoilt: the number of climbers visiting was not great enough to have a huge impact, and the ones that did come generally had a deep respect for the fragile environment. The more the years passed, the more I loved resting in such natural beauty. Simply watching the light change on the bark of a tree gave me pleasure, and going off alone with my camera was as much an excuse to find peace among the trees as it was to capture an image on film.

Later that afternoon Dave and I decided to descend to Chaltén to pick up food supplies for the mountain. Bruno and Laurence said they would come with us. The altimeter showed steady low pressure, so we could all relax and not worry about missing out on any stable weather. Without a heavy pack, the journey felt easy, and the thought of sinking our teeth into a steak after days of rice, lentils and soup spurred us on. Over a fine meal and a few ales we exchanged stories of people and mountains. Listening to Bruno and Laurence modestly describe their prolific adventures in Patagonia over the last few years, we realised that they were incredible mountaineers. Most of their stories involved a storm somewhere, and often it was a storm that robbed them of the summit. Yet rather than becoming bitter, they accepted storms as part of climbing here, something you could not fight. Just as important seemed their love of the landscape and the friends they had made.

The following morning the pressure on our altimeter remained low and so Dave and I decided to stay another night. Bruno and Laurence wanted to take a chance and returned to Rio Blanco with their packs full of food. That evening the stars shone brightly and the next day dawned clear and still. We walked back to our tent, then on past the lake and up to the col. By the time we reached the entrance to the snow cave, the wind was blowing and it had begun to snow. There was no sign of Bruno and Laurence, who were by now sharing the snow cave with us. In actual fact they were racing up Fitzroy. When they appeared the day after, they smiled, delirious from the effort but delighted they had reached the summit. We embraced them and then fed them copious cups of tea, good English tea. They had climbed in audacious style, with the bare minimum of equipment and clothing, a style that would frankly terrify even the most experienced alpinists. We listened, incredulous, as they recounted their ascent.

'It was difficult. The cracks have some ice and, higher, the wind began to increase. To save weight we left all our bivouac equipment behind and Laurence wore only rock shoes, no mountaineering boots or crampons, nothing like that.'

'How the hell did you climb the last part of the route up the ice fields to the summit?' Dave asked.

'Bruno climbed first and I came second with socks over my rock shoes.'

'I have never heard of anyone doing that before.'

'It worked well. My toes were a little cold but it saved us a lot of weight.'

'So where did you sleep last night?' I asked.

They began to laugh. 'It was awful, last night. We slept under the rocks near the Col de los Italianos, just this side, but it was very cold and windy. Not so good. No sleeping bags.' As Bruno spoke, I saw the exhaustion in his face, but contentment shone in his eyes.

Other than the classic snow route on Guillomet by Steph

and Charlie, very little had been achieved by anyone in recent weeks and this news gave everyone a boost. We were inspired by their daring and understood more fully what scale of commitment these peaks demanded.

For the next six days the weather remained terrible, with violent winds screaming down the glacier, and Dave and I lay mainly in the snow cave. Occasionally we battled through the storm down to the forest to save us going mad. 'The gap between dreams and reality in Patagonia is huge,' one climber had remarked. I understood the sentiment perfectly. I remembered a series of bizarre photographs shown to me by a Slovenian friend to illustrate the effects of Patagonian weather on the psyche. The first showed four well-built young men draped across an upright piano, dressed in nothing but their underpants. The group of normally mild-mannered climbers were returning from a long expedition to the menacing east face of Cerro Torre, and the piano belonged to the Slovenian Embassy Club in Buenos Aires, where the team were staying briefly before flying home. The celebratory drinks acted as a release for stress; stress induced by days of battling with the mountain in menacing storms. Eventually one of the Slovenians began leaping up and down, pounding the piano keys with his bare feet. The others soon followed suit, each man fighting for a chance to play the instrument. Finally, unable to withstand such persistent abuse, the piano collapsed. They were now blind drunk and decided to finish the job off good and proper. The final photograph showed little more than a heap of firewood and tangled wire on the floor of the embassy ballroom.

Having exhausted stories about ourselves and our friends, other curious topics of discussion arose in the cave, such as the debate on when brown sauce as opposed to tomato ketchup should be used. We agreed that a bacon sandwich was always tomato; bacon and egg, however, was brown. We couldn't say why.

As time passed, such fascinating subjects became harder to think of, and we found ourselves staring out of the snow cave and at our altimeters more and more frequently, like prisoners awaiting release. It seemed like we needed to achieve something so that we could justify leaving this treacherous place and going home to Christmas with our families.

We were desperate to climb our proposed new route. Each time we spied it through binoculars it had shed ice, slimming to a fraction of its original size.

'Soon it will have vanished altogether. It looks crazy, this climb,' Bruno had announced the previous week.

All along we had explained that this was precisely the style of climbing we enjoyed in Scotland, but now his comments had substance: the first 30 metres were completely bare, the ice having either collapsed or melted away.

'Once we're established on the wall, hopefully we'll be sheltered from the wind,' Dave began.

'Twenty-three bloody days we've been here, and apart from our flirt with Fitzroy, we've climbed one new pitch. Or should I say you have, I just held the ropes. I feel like I'm wasting away in this cave.'

'Maybe we should go tomorrow,' he enthused.

'What's it like out there now?'

'Hideous. Everybody else has gone down.'

I started to feel nauseous soon after the alarm sounded, an insidious feeling of sickness like on the morning of a dreaded school exam. I buried my face in the warmth of the sleeping bag. Dave's comment that he thought I had nothing to prove any more circled in my head. So why the hell was I lying here in this ice coffin about to do battle with the wind? At home, people would be immersed in the excitement of Christmas, buying gifts, drinking too much and listening to John Lennon. I thought of Elaine and what she would be doing. I hoped to God we could get this mountain climbed and return home in time for Christmas. I thought of my father's comment: 'The only use for bloody snow is on Christmas cards, I'll tell thee!' He hated it, as it served no purpose in his life. All it did was cause chaos on the roads, increase heating bills and prevent football matches being played. The petrol stove murmured, turning snow into hot water for tea, orange shadows dancing on the scalloped walls of the cave.

'Come on, Andy, time to get ready. I know you can't wait.'

'What's it like outside?'

'Clear, a bit breezy, but clear.'

We wriggled out of the tunnel just before 3 a.m., pushing our rucksacks in front of us. We cut a cube of snow-ice with the shafts of our ice axes and inserted it in the entrance behind us to stop any fresh snow blowing in. There had been a shovel outside for a while, tied to the cliff with a piece of rope, but eventually the wind had ripped it away, and all that remained was the frayed rope swaying in the breeze. Alone, we trod across the glacier, the sky lightening. It took a while for the muscles in our legs to warm, and I felt the wind whipping at my neck. Dave moved more quickly out in front. After an hour he paused, directly underneath the route that Andy Parkin had climbed solo. It tackled alarmingly steep ground in the central part. Up above, the sun burnt the edge of a large Zeppelin-shaped cloud.

'The Parkin reckoned he had relationship problems when he soloed that,' I said.

'Must have been heavy stuff. It looks insane.'

I moved in front to give Dave a rest, the snow deepening towards the base of our own climb, my lungs audible, sucking faster at the cold, sharp air. Wreaths of snow tumbled down the route, spilling on to a steep white soft cone almost 100 feet high. I glanced up, weakened by what I saw. A sudden wave of uncertainty overtook me. The climbing looked impossible; most of the ice had gone. I stared at my feet.

'What's the matter?'

'I'm not sure about this, Dave. It looks horrific.' I was halfway up the cone, a few minutes away from where the steep climbing began.

'Whatever you think, mate.'

Dave's gentleness only made it worse. It might have been easier if he had forced me to go on. Now I had to decide.

'Let's go down, Dave, it doesn't feel right,' I said, not wishing to prolong the horrible indecision.

Dave reversed back towards the base of the steep slope, which had taken 40 minutes to ascend. I followed. Once at the bottom, I stared back up.

'Maybe we should have had a look at it, at least have a go. What do you think?'

'Well, it's a long way to come to do nothing.'

'I know.'

'Let's give it a shot with a really small rucksack for the second climber. What's the worst that can happen?'

'I'm sorry for dithering,' I laughed. It was as if the normal mechanism for denying fear that mountaineers employ was malfunctioning. At least I had been able to be honest with Dave.

By the time we reached a junction in the route about 400 feet above the glacier, it started to snow; either that, or the constant spindrift pummelling down from above had become so intense that it felt like it was snowing. Snow had blown into the back of my hood and I could feel it melting around my neck as Dave's crampons scratched on the steep granite wall above. He knew he had to get established on the left system of iced corners if we were to have any chance. A small flake his crampon was resting on broke, and his full body weight shot on to his ice axes. I squeezed my gloved hands around the ropes, held my breath. He regained balance and decided to try a slightly higher traverse line. Occasionally he looked down, staring at how far he might fall. His shoulders faced the wall, his elbows down, locked tight. In everyday life Dave could be reserved, shy even, but scratching up ground like this brought out a different side in him: a quiet determination, as if instinct-ively stalking his prey. As he edged away from me, the belief in his craft was unmistakable. It travelled down the icy rope to my hands, rebuilding my own belief. The excitement, the uncertainty, the grace in the danger, I sensed it now, and with it I felt the numbness fade. Maybe I had something to prove after all, if only to myself.

He waved his arms to signal he had made it and started taking in the rope.

'Great lead,' I said, finally joining him, pumped from gripping the ice axes too tightly.

'Thanks. Look up above.'

I glanced up quickly and then turned away as the blood returned to my hands. I felt sick. I eased my fingers from the ends of the gloves with my teeth and made a fist. The pain of hot aches never got any easier to bear.

'That steep corner?'

'There's nowhere else to go.'

A short wall led up to the base of the corner, where I hammered in a peg, each blow sounding like a lone dull church bell. I clipped in the rope and stood up, my crampon points quivering on a thin horizontal intrusion of black rock. I stretched and swung my axes into thin ice at the base of the corner proper and stood on a small ledge. For the next 60 feet, the walls of the corner looked totally smooth, no chance for protection. I craned my head back; the white ice, a foot wide and three or four inches thick, soared up out of sight. I moved gingerly but steadily until 40 feet above the ledge, trying to remain calm, consciously regulating my breathing. Here the ice had thinned out and no longer stuck to the wall, so that when my ice axe struck, I detected an ugly, hollow sound. The ice had narrowed to just six inches wide, perhaps two inches thick in the centre, which meant one axe had to be placed directly above the other in the centre of the streak. The angle had increased, and I felt my arms fading. Falling was not an option. I desperately needed a more comfortable position, more secure ice. I made one more move, and a crack sounded. Jesus. The ice had started to collapse under my feet. I glanced down and saw only bare rock. No way back. One foothold of ice remained, the size of an ice cream. I stabbed at it with my toe, but it flew off down towards Dave. I stared at the two precious ice axe placements, the thin line between here and darkness. My heart quickened.

I had a few seconds to do something, anything. A bad plan

is better than no plan, I remembered the teacher telling us at the school chess club. Move, and move fast. I had to be considerate too, otherwise the upper ice would go. I placed both crampon points on ripples in the granite and then lifted the tip of my right axe from the ice and gently struck higher. It held. I sank my body downwards, placing some weight on it, testing. It wasn't great, but I worried that if I struck again I might rip the whole lot off. My forearms were burning. I felt the grip of my hands loosening around the metal shafts. I was slipping. I stared left and then right. Nothing. The walls of a prison cell. The only escape was up. Desperate, I pressed my shoulders out on to each side of the corner, trying to ease the weight from the axes, attempting to breathe life into my swollen arms. But I heard the fabric of my jacket slithering down. In a flash I jumped the sole of my foot behind me so that all crampon points bit into the rock, and then let my knee jam on the opposite wall. That's the baby, I muttered. I had never done it before, but the manoeuvre worked; at last I got the weight off my arms. It was skill, luck and madness. Life in the old dog yet, I thought, and set off towards a thicker piece of ice, edging nearer and nearer towards the safety of a small ledge and a place to fix the rope.

'Good effort, mate. That was hard.'

'Cheers. I didn't have a choice really.'

'We should eat and drink something. We haven't stopped for twelve hours.'

To the east the hills had lost the earlier sun, and they faded gloomily into the plains and the fuzzy horizon beyond. Thick cloud swirled above our heads now, and the wind had increased. We had brought no sleeping bags or any other equipment to spend a night out. We had no choice but to keep going. Snow blasted down the wall like cold sugar, sticking to my face. Up above, Dave chopped at the ice, small chunks rattling straight down and bouncing off my helmet and then into the void.

We followed the steep, thin white snake of ice through remarkable scenery for 1200 feet until we were below a 200-foot overhanging chimney crack. Night was near; you could smell it. Dave started up without speaking; we were too exhausted for words. The jaws of the crack were only wide enough for one shoulder. After two hours of effort he stopped beneath a giant mushroom of ice. A maelstrom had shrouded us and thicker snow began surging down the chimney, threatening to flush us off the face.

Dave stood with his feet in étriers on a wall of granite as smooth as glass, his whole body weight and mine hanging from two small nuts he had hammered into a vertical icy seam a centimetre wide.

'I couldn't find anything else,' he said, seeing my expression when I joined him.

'That was pretty extreme out there climbing. We can't be far from the summit.'

'Very close, I reckon, but it's going to be dark soon, it's ten o'clock. Let's get the head torches out.'

Snow cascaded down the climb, freezing our eyelashes together. To save weight we'd brought just one duvet jacket. I passed it to Dave. I warmed my hands by slapping them together and then set off, climbing for 30 feet, searching for ice thick enough to take an ice screw but with no luck. Instead I headed over to a wide crack and tried to place a large camming device; it wouldn't fit. I would have to climb the enormous ice bulge with no protection, which meant that if I did fall, I would shock-load the belay. The thought made me tense. I hooked my ice axe around a small column of ice, moved my feet up and then smashed the other axe up above. I released one foot and then transferred weight to the upper arm. Suddenly I was blinded.

'Watch me here, Dave!' I screamed, but the words were lost in the torrent of snow that tried to tear my head from my shoulders.

'Dave, watch me . . .'

The upper axe started to cut through the ice. I was sliding.

My heart pumped harder, faster. I opened one eye; the other had frozen over in the chaos. The axe bit again and I turned my head down to stare at Dave. My mind raced. Even if I survived a 70-foot fall, what was to say I wouldn't take him with me, the pair of us plummeting down to the glacier?

Tiring rapidly, I managed to reverse back down to the belay.

'I can't make it, Dave, I'm sorry.' I felt defeated, my spirit crushed.

'It looks horrible.'

'I tried my best. I nearly fell there, that snow was pushing me off.' I shone my head torch at Dave.

'You can't afford to fall. Besides, it's so late. We've got to get down yet. I don't think we'd survive the night up here. Look at the weather.'

It had started to snow thick and fast now, and the wind buffeted us. I knew it was over.

Dave abseiled first, his crampons screeching over the rock like the claws of a steel cat, snow swirling down, the light of his head torch gliding into gloom. Twenty minutes later, once he had a belay, I felt the ropes slacken. I shone my head torch at my groin, checking my harness buckle and belay device twice, and then descended. It would be so easy to die abseiling. To survive you had to fight the sleep, ignore the temptation to panic or to rush. A game of chess where stale-mate doesn't exist, every decision we make requiring respect and rationale.

At around midnight, dangling together 600 feet above the glacier, the storm intensified. Dave aimed his light at a crack, trying to clear it of snow before placing an extra metal chock to abseil from, but tumbling powder snow drowned us. It would stop for a few seconds then thud on my helmet and shoulders, startling me each time, setting my heart racing. I hung on the rope and tried to lie horizontally, acting as a canopy above Dave, taking the brunt of the snow slides so that he could build the anchors required to get the hell out of here. We had moved beyond pain now, beyond hunger.

Thirty long minutes passed before Dave had fixed the anchor. I clipped in next to him. He cut off a length of abseil tape, then held the knife between his teeth, using both hands to tie a knot in the tape. He threaded the ropes, tied them together and then bounced his body weight on it before committing to it. An updraught powered snow into my nostrils, stinging. My jacket had frozen into a suit of iced armour; only a light crease at the elbows and knees allowed movement.

'I like it here. I might come here for my holidays,' I joked, hoping to squeeze out another burst of concentration.

'Yes, it's great, isn't it.' Dave smiled, ice sheathing the hood of his jacket glistening in the beam of my light.

The relief of finally feeling my feet on the glacier left me giddy. We hadn't reached the summit, but we had survived. All we had to do now was find the snow hole. That morning I had taken a bearing with my compass and we followed it now, stumbling in the dark, our legs sinking into impossibly deep snow. We found the entrance to our snow cave as the dawn sky lightened, exactly 24 hours after setting off. We crawled into our sleeping bags and vanished into bottomless sleep.

The forest had lost none of its charm, but we were oblivious to it. Our failure hurt us, a deep itch; the more you questioned and scratched at it, the worse it became. Should I have tried harder? Should we have carried more clothes so that we could have slept out? Should we have tried to set off a few days earlier before the ice had shrunk so much?

We had pushed ourselves to the limit, physically and psychologically, and yet we couldn't relax properly in the forest. After packing our equipment, we left a pile of bags by the cabin that hopefully Guerra would come and get with his horses. We said goodbye to everyone and walked down towards Chaltén.

Dave regularly checked his altimeter and then stared over his shoulder up at the mountain, bitterness in his face.

'I bet we were less than sixty metres from the summit,' he said. 'It would have been good to stand on top.'

I agreed, but tried to placate him. 'We had done the meat of it. And it's not as if anyone else has been doing new routes.

We could have done the regular route on Poincenot, but it wouldn't have been such hard climbing. That's the gamble we took.'

It was late by the time we reached the edge of Chaltén.

'I think we are better sleeping out tonight; the weather looks OK.'

'Let's try behind the boulder,' suggested Dave.

We groped around in the dark, searching for a flat piece of grass. I placed my sleeping bag on the ground and used my jacket as a pillow. We lay under the stars, silent. I understood now why Andy Parkin and so many other mountaineers returned repeatedly to Patagonia. I needed to thank Andy and Agostini for inspiring me and rekindling my passion for serious mountaineering. During my stay here, I had felt a deep connection with elemental wildness. The weather was undeniably savage, but the beauty and sense of space were extraordinary. We had pushed ourselves on the climbs and worked well as a team, and I think we both knew that one day we would return. There were so many summits to explore and so much history to try and unravel.

Though I felt disappointed, I had reason to be pleased. I had returned to the mountains and committed myself. I had overcome my fear of failure by failing.

'Have you ever seen a sky as beautiful as that?' I said after a few minutes. I gazed up at the Southern Cross and the Magellanic Clouds, and then fell into a deep sleep.

6

Travels with The Fly

Patagonia had been a mixture of pleasure and pain and it hadn't answered all of my questions about how I felt about mountains. I loved being back in the wild, and I had enjoyed Dave's company, but I still felt unsure about mountaineering. Meanwhile, I missed the joy of movement over rock. The chance of a trip to Norway arose with a bunch of the wild young climbing Turks, which sounded fun and a good antidote to the trips to India and Patagonia. Our plan was to explore the fabled big walls rising out of the Lysefjord in south-western Norway, but the diabolical weather meant that we never even saw the place. Instead, for a fortnight we found ourselves paying extortionate prices for beer, racing around in an Alfa Romeo and concluding that it would have been much cheaper for us to fly to California and climb there, where the sun always shone.

Without doubt the most notable ascent occurred back in Newcastle, when Leo Houlding, aka The Fly, disgruntled at not being able to leave his imprint on Norwegian climbing history, decided to levitate up Antony Gormley's Angel of the North. Leo climbed the 20-metre steel sculpture solo without ropes and then proceeded to walk along the 54-metre wings. Sadly, because the Angel sits right next to the A1, the authorities were notified immediately.

'A man is trying to kill himself,' drivers screamed down their phones to the police while steering with one hand.

Leo was arrested and left to explain himself to the Geordie nation on local TV that night and then to the rest of the nation via the tabloid press the following morning.

Cecil Slingsby, the Englishman who explored the mountains of Norway prolifically during the latter half of the nineteenth century, became known as 'the grandfather of Norwegian mountaineering'. He referred to 'the kindness and gentle attentions' of the people he met, and called the land 'one of our great playgrounds'. Despite the awful weather, this same combination of people and potential adventure loomed large in my mind. Intrigued by what I had heard whispered of the Lysefjord, I decided to return with the youngest and wildest of the young Turks – The Fly. Teenager Leo had been tearing up the climbing scene with outrageously bold ascents on UK rock and a mind-boggling ascent of El Nino, one of the hardest climbs on El Capitan in Yosemite, California. To Leo, I might not have been the grandfather of British mountaineering, but he did frequently refer to me as 'the old man'.

Leo arrived at Sheffield railway station with a large ghetto-blaster in hand. The volume was so high that the platform sounded like a nightclub on Saturday night. Inside the Newcastle-bound train, the volume unaltered, the entire carriage of passengers stared at us. Leo revelled in the attention. I hid behind my book, like an ineffectual elder.

'Do you fancy a cup of tea?'

'You what?' he shouted.

'Tea?' I yelled.

'Lager, get me a lager.'

I did as I was told, not sure whether he was legally old enough to drink.

On returning from the buffet, shocked by the noise screeching from his music box, I prepared to apologise to the other passengers. However, when I looked around I noticed at least two groups of young girls swaying and clicking their fingers in time to the beat, and trying to catch Leo's attention.

The relief of finally exiting the carriage at Newcastle was short-lived. After less than five minutes, Leo decided to roll his 30-kilo haul bag full of ropes and climbing equipment along the floor, kicking it whenever it slowed.

As we approached the top of a long, steep ramp leading to the underground, I queried the safety of this system, suggesting it might be better if he carried it.

'The problem is, mate, I'm naturally lazy,' he replied.

Just then an old lady appeared below us from a side entrance. The bag accelerated towards the back of her legs like a deadly tumbling block of granite.

'Arggg! Fuck! Shit! Arggg!' screamed Leo, dropping the ghetto-blaster and leaping down the ramp, desperate to halt the bag. 'Watch out!'

The woman did not react to his yelling; perhaps she was deaf.

I held my breath, expecting carnage. Leo pounced on the bag as if arresting a runaway thief. The woman continued walking, oblivious.

'Oh my God, that was close. That was really dumb,' he said, in a rare moment of self-criticism.

'You are very lucky, the weather is perfect,' our good buddy Trym told us at Stavanger airport.

We joined our friends Sindre and Elizabeth for dinner, and then the Arctic explorer Rolf Boer arrived, bearing a bottle of whisky. Excited at the prospect of climbing big new routes in the Lysefjord, Leo drank at a furious pace. Later we took a stroll down to the harbour and Leo began honing his skills on a neighbouring wooden house, lay-backing up an arête, then leaping and clasping the windowsill with both hands before pulling himself up. A startled elderly couple stared at him from the other side of the glass. His arms tired soon enough, and he fell to the ground and ran away.

*   *   *

Rolf kindly offered to lend us his car, an old Fiat Panda, for the trip, so the following morning we filled it with food and our climbing equipment. Without warning, Leo produced an Alfa Romeo badge from his wallet and proudly stuck it on the bonnet of the Fiat with plumber's tape.

'Nicked it from Neil's car,' he smiled, referring to the motor we'd careered around in on our trip the previous year. He then plugged in the ghetto-blaster and, after donning shades, we left Stavanger in search of the fabled fjord.

The sun beat down from a cloudless sky as we headed out towards the mountains. The 'Fiat Romeo' coughed and spluttered a little on the steeper hills but moved along well enough, weaving through the vast unspoilt valleys of Rogaland; a landscape virtually devoid of human life, a place peopled by cliffs and remote lakes. Stripped to our waists, we marvelled at this emptiness and the work of prehistoric glaciers that had carved and smoothed the golden rocks that rose everywhere from the greenery. As the day wore on, more and more pristine cliffs appeared; only our desire to see the fjord kept us from stopping and trying to climb them.

'And there are so few climbers!' Leo remarked.

'There are probably more people driving around London on the M25 right now than even live in Norway.'

During the middle of the nineteenth century, vast numbers of people abandoned Norway for America as treaties with Indians in the Midwest were opening up land for white farm settlers. Escaping from Norway's rigid social class system and gaining the right to vote were motivations very attractive to the average Norwegian, plus the economic benefits were huge, with craftsmen making four dollars a day as opposed to fifty dollars a year back home. The rate of migration out of Norway didn't really slow until the 1930s, when economic stability returned. One of the most famous inhabitants of the Lysefjorden was a vagabond nicknamed Limping Joe (Pilt-Ola). He decided to try and walk to America through Russia and then Siberia. Joe returned to Lysefjorden, his mission a failure, but he had given it a good go, having been on the move for seven years. One can only imagine that his limp had worsened after such an outing. Nowadays the Lysefjorden has only a handful of families living there, along with a few workers who look after the hydro-electric power plant at Lyseboten.

The hydro-scheme was the reason for the amazing road that now dropped via countless hairpins down to the water's edge. The moment we caught our first glimpse of the immaculate walls of the fjord, Leo turned up the music and leaned out of the car yelling: 'All right. All right. All right!'

We parked the car and stood still, astonished by the vista. The surface of the water shone like marble, a still aqua-green sheet that stretched for 16 kilometres. On each side cliffs plunged into the fjord, barely a kilometre between them, but it was the left-hand walls of Kjerag that seized our attention. Almost 1000 metres high, blank and overhanging in parts, it was as if the Yosemite Valley had been flooded.

'If the weather stays like this, we're going to tear this place apart.'

'I think you're right, Leo,' I replied nervously.

More than 50 tents filled the campsite, comprising a few walkers but almost exclusively base jumpers. Significantly more dangerous than skydiving, base jumping involves leaping from fixed objects with a parachute. The acronym 'BASE' stands for the four categories of recognised fixed objects: buildings; antennae, such as aerial masts; spans, bridges or arches; and earth, cliffs or other natural formations, such as Kjerag. A dozen or so people had their chutes spread out on the grass, and were carefully packing them ready for action. In the distance one guy stood in a yellow suit with webbed sections under the arms and between his legs; a sort of cross between a clown and Batman. After putting up our tent, we started organising our climbing equipment, coiling our ropes and clipping karabiners on to camming devices. This brought a lot of attention from those camped around us. People stared as though we had leprosy. Rather unusually, we were the oddballs of the campsite.

'Hey, where you guys from?' a long-haired man asked as he passed with a folded chute under his arm.

'Britain.'

'Cool. You're climbers, right?'

'Yes.'

'Well you certainly got a lot of stuff.'

'And you?'

'I'm Norwegian. I jump. I mean, shit, why spend days fighting gravity up that wall when I can fly past it in twelve seconds?' He started laughing.

'I see your logic. It must be a hell of a buzz.'

'It's pretty good. You guys want to come over to drink tea when you've sorted your stuff out? I live in that caravan over there in the corner.'

After finishing packing, we ate supper and watched Kris demonstrate a variety of flying poses to a group of four fledgling base jumpers on the grass outside his caravan. From a distance you could have been forgiven for thinking they were practising yoga, balanced as they were on one leg with arched backs and both hands in the air. The difference, of course, was that early the next morning they would be trying to hold this position whilst travelling at 200 miles per hour, head first, praying that the 6lb bag of nylon strapped to their backs was going to open correctly.

Later, in the caravan sipping tea, Kris radiated a deep calm. Behind him, every inch of the wall was plastered with postcards of cliffs, buildings, bridges and radio towers.

'Friends keeping me up to date with their activities, you know.'

I lifted up a card; on the front was a tall red antenna mast, on the reverse the words 'Hi Kris, jumped this mother. Great trip, man!' Another was a photo of a huge hotel in Singapore: 'Got free accommodation for the weekend after jumping this devil for a publicity stunt! Take it easy, bro.' Now I understood a little of what people felt like when they came round to our house and stared at all the postcards of Himalayan peaks pinned above the breakfast table in the kitchen.

'I'd love to fly,' said Leo.

'On the other side of the fjord we have a place where you can learn. It's a static line so your chute opens automatically and it's above the water so it's safe. You should try it, guys.'

Until the mid-1990s, Kjerag was virtually unknown except within a few small circles of adventurous climbers either side of the North Sea. Local Rogaland climbers climbed the first recorded route in 1980, but it was the audacious Pat Littlejohn who breached the central wall of Kjerag five years later. Despite a couple of other ascents by Norwegian climbers, it took a base jumper to put the place on the map. The moment Norwegian Stein Edvardsen leapt in 1994, everything changed, and soon this was *the* place to base jump. This stirred the climbers into action, and many superb routes were established. The Shield in particular had an aura. The magnificent upper blank wall, overhanging entirely, had provided difficult aid climbing. Pat Littlejohn had mentioned to me that he believed The Shield would be a sensational free climb.

Though the campsite overflowed with base jumpers keen to fly into the fjord, it remained a serious proposition, with deaths almost every year. People from America, Australia, Italy, Russia, Sweden and France have had their lives cut short at the foot of Kjerag. The famous James Bond stuntman, Britain's Terry Forrestal, died base jumping here.

We left Kris in the caravan and walked back to our tent. A few people were still packing their chutes in the late light. Kris had not mentioned that his best friend, Thor Alex Kappfjell, one of the most experienced base jumpers in the world, had died flying off Kjerag just a few days earlier.

The next day we had planned to set off and attempt to free-climb the route Hoka Hey, a steep 800-metre grey wall, split by a system of relentless cracks. However, we learnt that our plans had been leaked within the small Norwegian climbing community and a strong local team had been sent in advance to compete with us. Miraculously, the Norwegians were one full day ahead, having spent the previous night sleeping halfway up the wall. In some ways we took their action as a compliment; they obviously felt threatened by a couple of foreign rogues who had sailed over to raid their jewels.

'Bloody Vikings!' I said. 'They are everywhere.'

'Well at least they're not on The Shield,' said Leo. 'We need to be first on that.'

'Maybe we should follow on behind them. Hoka Hey looks like a great route anyhow.'

'It's a pain in the arse.'

'Totally, but we need to get a route under our belts before tackling The Shield.'

'We need to be the first on The Shield,' Leo said. 'But OK, let's start with Hoka.'

Leaving the campsite that afternoon, adorned in helmets, harnesses, karabiners and coiled ropes, we received quizzical looks from the base jumpers. Down on the shoreline, a Californian man named Tracey waited for us in a small boat. Twice a day, jumpers drove up the hairpins and then marched along to Kjerag's various takeoff points, and Tracey's business was to collect them from the landing site and bring them back to Lyseboten. He said very little, wore sunglasses and a blue bandanna around his long hair.

'It's complicated,' he said, when I asked him how he had ended up in a place like this. I wondered about the story, whether it was love or something else.

The water wrapped around the bow of the boat like thick molten glass as we powered past walls that rose cathedral-like into the sky. They were so tall that it hurt your neck to look. The top of Kjerag had disappeared into a thick layer of cloud that had moved in from lower down the fjord. Tracey cut the engine and we glided to a stop.

'K6 to base, over.'

'Base here.'

'How's it looking from down there?'

'It's looking bad, dude. There's a cloud inversion that's dropping lower.'

'What height is the cloud base sitting at?'

'Hard to say, but it's not good, I'm telling you.' Tracey looked agitated.

'OK, we'll wait up here.'

'You could be waiting a long time, dude.'

'That's OK.'

'Don't these guys ever learn?' Tracey said to us, pointing at the slope of grass and rocks. 'Just last week a guy died right there, jumping into shit like this.'

'They get disorientated, yes?' Leo asked.

'Right. They don't know what height they are at and pull too late. It's all fucked up. That guy that died, man, he was supposed to be one of the best base jumpers in the world.'

On the back of the boat Tracey had a small fishing rod, but he didn't look in the mood for fishing. I put my hand over the side, dropped my fingers into the still, cold water. It looked deep here, and staring around, it was difficult to imagine the scale of those ancient grinding glaciers.

In most countries to skydive you need a licence, which is examined before you are allowed into the aircraft. In the UK you need a licence for everything, to ride a moped or to fish on a canal. Yet anyone can go out and buy base jumping gear and get to work. A new chute costs around £2000, and unlike skydiving, you don't need a plane to haul you into the sky. Throw on something to keep the wind off, a decent pair of sunglasses to stop your eyes watering, choose your spot and off you go. In fact, compared to the cost of our climbing gear currently filling the front half of Tracey's boat, base jumping kit was cheap and less cumbersome.

'OK, base, we're coming.'

We stared up at the thick cloud, and a few seconds later two black shapes rocketed out of the underbelly, large wingless birds careering straight towards us.

Tracey pursed his lips and shook his head. He started the boat and we glided towards the small spur of grass and rocks. Leo and I disembarked, shook hands with Tracey and set off towards the base of the wall, where the men now stood, their chutes half full of air like giant marshmallows on the ground behind them.

After just a few minutes' walk, we stumbled upon a patch of grass covered in flowers, empty beer cans and cigarette butts. Up above, voices sounded; it was the two Norwegian climbers somewhere on the wall.

'This must be where that guy died last week,' Leo said. 'There's obviously been a wake here for him.'

I paused and nodded without saying anything, then we carried on, sweating as the hillside steepened. Defiant plants and small trees were managing to survive, clinging to the first 200 feet of cliff, until the rock emerged cleaner and steeper, with just a few small mosses lingering in some of the cracks. Traces of chalk from the hands of the Norwegians made finding our way easier, and the rock itself gave just enough holds with a surprising roughness. It seemed stupid that the only two teams of climbers in the whole of the relatively unexplored fjord were on the same climb. We had been given two or three sketch drawings of routes that would be good to try and make first free ascents of, and we had focused on these. Having people in front of us wasn't ideal, but now, absorbed in the movement, we forgot about them.

'What's the plan, old man?'

We had arrived at an obvious place to sleep, a wide ledge covered in ferns, grass and tiny yellow flowers.

'Well we might as well use these ferns to make a mattress, then we can lay ropes over the top and we'll have a comfy little set-up.'

An hour later we had two places big enough to lie down. I gave Leo the spare thick socks and a bivvy bag and then jumped into the sleeping bag.

'Hold on,' he said. 'What do you think you're doing?'

'I'm going to bed. We've got a lot of climbing to do tomorrow.'

'How come you're in the sleeping bag?' He sounded exasperated.

'Well you can have it tomorrow.'

'I thought you were a tough, hairy-arsed mountaineer.'

'Age before beauty, friend. My bones are aching a bit these days. It won't bother a young lad like you.'

'I don't believe this.' He was visibly sulking. 'Wait till I get back home. I'm going to tell everybody you're a fake.'

The very last of the sun lit his face and the whites of his saddened eyes stared at me almost comically from beneath the helmet. He'd fixed the Alfa badge to this and it was still stuck there.

'Are you still whingeing? You want to get in the bivvy bag, otherwise you'll get cold.'

He tucked his trousers into the socks and then got into the bag, resting his back against the wall. He lit a cigarette and blew smoke down towards the water, 1000 feet below. The air in the fjord cooled as the sky darkened and moisture gathered in the leaves of the ferns on the ledge.

'It's my birthday as well tomorrow,' he said.

'How old are you?'

'Nineteen.'

'Happy birthday, mate. Make the most of your teens, it's all downhill after that,' I laughed.

'What a birthday, not even got a sleeping bag.'

'For Christ's sake, will you shut up? I'm trying to sleep over here.'

The next morning, above the ledge, my legs pushed out against the smooth walls of a steep groove. I strained, trying to place a tiny brass wire in a hairline crack before swinging out right towards a ledge, a place I might be able to stop and belay. Abruptly, a noise shattered the calm; my immediate thought was rock fall. My head shrank into my torso and I closed my eyes, but the noise got louder. I leaned back and saw a missile falling. Nervously, I pushed the wire into the crack and clipped in the rope before my legs weakened. Quick of breath, I managed to get my feet on to better footholds and then stared at Leo.

'What the hell . . . ?'

Leo smiled and pointed to the sky. Suddenly another shape

rushed past. It sounded like a large plastic bag half filled with bricks, chucked off a bridge. I held my breath until the meteor had passed. And then another; this body whooped as it hurtled past. Finally someone floated by doing controlled somersaults incredibly close to the wall, their feet strapped to a yellow surf-board. We thought it might have been Kris.

Now the chutes were opening and swaying just above the water. I made it up on to the small ledge and tied off my ropes.

'Climb when you're ready,' I yelled down, and then took off my helmet. My hair was wet through, as much from the fear of watching the flying bodies as the effort of climbing.

'OK, climbing,' shouted Leo.

Our sport seemed laughably slow and ordered compared to what we had just witnessed. We were a couple of snails inching our way up the wall, relying on the rock to offer edges and cracks so that we could move some more. No wonder they thought we were weird.

'One of them looked like a total punter. Did you see?'

'I wasn't watching that closely, to be honest.'

'He fell like a rag doll.'

'One of them was actually flying out towards the water.'

'Yes, that looked fun, man. I want a go.'

Though never ridiculous, the climbing was tough and sustained, and we could see where the Norwegians in front had removed small plants from cracks in order to insert their fingers. Most of the rock was dry, but less than a couple of hundred feet from the top, we found ourselves below an evil, wet, wide crack. I liked crack climbing, but just above the halfway point, I felt my arms swell and realised that I must hurry if I was going to succeed.

'Watch me here, Leo,' I shouted, feeling the skin on the back of my hands slide and tear. Blood mixed with the black slime that oozed from the rock. Just a few more feet and I've done it, I told myself.

'Go on, Cavey,' Leo yelled.

I managed to crawl on to the grassy ledge, euphoric but

feeling nauseous. I could see the top of the cliff clearly now. Leo came up the crack, cursing each time his hands slipped: he hated cracks. It was a rare thing to see him struggle.

'Well done, old man,' he said, joining me. 'That was hard.'

We arrived on top to be greeted by Dag Hagen and Lars Terjesen.

'We had to restore some Norwegian pride. I'm sure you understand.' Dag laughed.

We shook each other's hands, our knuckles scarred and bloody from the final crack. Just a few yards away was the main jumping exit point. We went over and Leo held on to the short rope fixed there, his body hanging above the abyss.

'I'm mad for it,' he yelled into the void.

And I knew he meant it. A few months earlier, in Yosemite, he had walked to the top of the biggest cliff, El Capitan, and, with a 200-foot slack rope attached to his waist, dived off. He enjoyed it so much he did it again. He wasn't someone easily frightened.

Early the following morning, an American man appeared outside our tent.

'Excuse me, you guys the climbers?'

My eyes were glued together and my arms felt like lead.

'That's us,' Leo groaned, before sticking his head out of the tent.

'We have a buddy stuck up there in the trees below the K1 jumping site.'

Before I knew it, Leo was up, dressed and gone.

The K1 jump, known colloquially as a 'hop and pop' jump, is the shortest of the eight official exits used by the base jumpers. The cliff at this point is only vertical for 250 feet or so. Throw a stone off and it will hit the ground in just three seconds. Jumpers leap with their chutes already open in their hands so that they inflate immediately – every one of those three seconds counts.

One of the worst things that can happen to a base jumper is a 'one-eighty', where the chute opens 180 degrees the wrong way, meaning the pilot is spun back towards the structure he or she has jumped from. Canopies have a front and a back, and air filling the front is what stabilises the chute. There are three main causes of a one-eighty, the most common being an asymmetrical body position. The art of flying relies on good body alignment, especially a straight spine. Another hazard is when a crosswind hits the unweighted chute and spins it around. Finally, chutes have to be packed correctly to avoid opening back-to-front. An experienced flyer will normally be able to extricate himself from such a predicament, having spent hours practising an automatic response. Less experienced flyers, who might not appreciate what is happening, could find themselves heading for the ground at terminal velocity. It stands to reason that shorter jumps are more dangerous.

By the time I got up, quite a crowd had huddled in the centre of the campsite and binoculars were being passed around. I went over and had a look.

Leo scrambled down a steep rocky gully until he was directly above the shouting Texan. He had suffered a one-eighty and landed in a tree, uninjured but unable to climb out. Had he crashed into the cliff he would have been seriously injured or killed. Leo abseiled 400 feet and found the man stuck in the tree, his chute tangled above him. Embarrassed at having to be rescued, he spoke gruffly but managed to climb out with the aid of a rope. That afternoon an older American man came over and left six beers outside our tent as a thank-you.

'Well done, youth,' I said, opening one of the bottles. 'I've got a terrible thirst after watching you up there.'

For a couple of days we explored cliffs close to the campsite and had fun playing on some giant boulders, but soon enough our attentions turned back to Kjerag. Agreeing that we needed to do one more climb before heading up on to The Shield, we attempted a route called Fjord Cruise, a tenuous line of thin cracks just right of a constant waterfall. It looked a tough proposition, and we decided to take a heavier big-wall approach, with more food and equipment, including a portaledge, bottles of water and a sleeping bag each. This style is inevitably slower and involves a lot of hard work lifting the haul bag up the climb, but it does mean you have the time to deal with potentially difficult sections or to sit out bad weather.

As we dragged the bag laboriously up the lower easy section, I found myself staring more and more at the cascading waterfall, worried that rocks might be mixed with the water and convinced that if a wind picked up, it could be redirected on to our heads. A third of the way up the wall, we discovered a small cave and took refuge under a darkening sky. Local legend has it that when the wind and the rain come from the south-east, pressure builds up in the cracks and chimneys of Smell-Veggen, a cliff next to Kjerag, and it gives off an almighty bang. The bang we heard, though, sounded suspiciously like thunder, and before long the whole fjord turned into what the author Victor Hugo described when he visited it as a 'most terrible corridor of all the world seas'. Lying on a metal-framed portaledge inside a cave, suspended from two alloy wedges in a crack and surrounded by metal climbing equipment during a lightning storm didn't bode well. We survived the lightning, but by the following morning water was cascading down the wall and starting to run into the cave.

'I don't like this, Leo.'

'I don't think it's going to clear.'

'I'm worried we'll get trapped here. Look at the size of that waterfall below us.'

'It's not that bad.'

'If it gets any bigger, it will cover our descent route. I don't fancy drowning.'

Leo thought I was overreacting but agreed we should descend. We packed up all our gear into the haul bag. Nervous, wearing all the clothes I had, I went out into the tempest. Whilst arranging the first abseil, I turned around to spot Leo standing on a small ledge above the roof of the cave, water bouncing off his head and shoulders. He had both hands inside his jacket and was fiddling around his stomach area. He looked utterly relaxed.

'Leo, don't stand there in the firing line, you're freaking me out. Come over here, it's safer,' I shouted. 'We need to get out of here.'

'Hold on, will you,' he shouted back. 'I'm just rolling a fag.'

7

Lord of the skies

Everything in Lyseboten turned gold. It was the sun returning at last. The base jumpers emerged from their tents and began inspecting and packing their chutes. Towards the back of the campsite, the BBC was filming a tall, long-haired, peculiarly dressed Englishman called Adrian. Adrian stood in a brightly coloured nylon suit, his limbs splayed, revealing taut fabric between his legs and between his torso and arms. His girlfriend Katarina studied the outfit, and together they discussed ways of making it more efficient for flying.

'These are the guys I was telling you about,' said David, the Welsh filmmaker, as we approached.

'You're the crazy climbers, right?' Adrian asked softly. 'It looks pretty extreme on that cliff from what I've seen of it.'

I felt flattered that a man attempting to fly from a 1000-metre cliff, dressed in a modified shellsuit, considered us crazy.

'Excuse my ignorance, what the hell are you wearing?' I asked awkwardly, intrigued yet sensing that we were perhaps interrupting an important technical discussion.

'This is a webbed wingsuit,' said David. 'We're hoping to film Adrian flying in the fjord.'

'It looks radical. Do you carry a reserve chute?' asked Leo.

'Most people don't, but actually I do.'

'I would want at least two, maybe three or four,' I said.

The previous summer Adrian had watched in horror as his friend and mentor, Patrick de Gayardon, had plunged to his death attempting to become the first man to fly. Gayardon had been unable to open either of his chutes. Instead of abandoning the quest, Adrian had decided to continue where his friend had left off. Just a few months before visiting Kjerag, after making some modifications to the suit, he had broken the world records for time and distance, though he almost died in the escapade. He had jumped from an aeroplane 38,850 feet above California; 10,000 feet higher than the summit of Mount Everest. With temperatures as low as minus 120 degrees centigrade, the return valve of his oxygen mask froze and he was unable to exhale. Close to losing consciousness, he managed to break the seal slightly by screwing up his face and found he could breathe shallowly. He flew for four minutes 55 seconds and travelled 10 miles, setting new world records for the longest skydive and the furthest flight by man. Suddenly Doc Moseley's antics in the gyrocopter and aeroplane, which had so horrified me, seemed insignificant.

Adrian and Katarina looked preoccupied, so we wished them the best of luck and wandered back.

'If you see us up on the wall, wave to us as you nip past,' I joked. 'There are no other climbers now, so we're easy to spot.'

That evening we found Tracey and hitched a ride down the fjord. A few days earlier, we had driven up a small road directly opposite Kjerag and traced the line of The Shield through binoculars. A kilometre high, the tower rises out of the fjord from a strip of dense green forest. A system of steep corners and cracks leads to a tiny ledge at half-height, but the heart of the route centres around the golden shield of rock higher up that gives the climb its name. During the first ascent, our friend Morton Diesen had free-climbed the first 10 pitches, but had negotiated the blankest section using skyhooks, pieces of hardened steel, bent like buttoning hooks and about the width of a fingernail. These can be placed over tiny flakes of granite. A foot loop is attached to each skyhook and – praying that the tiny flakes of rock do not tear from the wall – the climber balances up. We, however, were aiming to free-climb, and would be hanging from these tiny flakes by our fingers. Morton had assured us that a small crack split the 1200-foot overhanging sweep of granite, but we struggled to locate it that day.

Now, as The Shield came into view, it looked even steeper and more featureless than I remembered, and an endless queue of questions began nagging at me. Were we good enough? What would happen if the weather changed? What if one of us fell and got bashed up? Was *I* good enough?

We bivouacked in a cave beneath a giant boulder and I cooked a large meal of pasta; cooking took my mind off the climb. I normally hated washing up, but after the meal I did the dishes, I needed to be busy. Was the dread I had felt in Patagonia returning? I knew The Shield wouldn't have the dangers inherent in mountaineering, but there was potential to take huge, bone-breaking falls. Perhaps it was simply the fear of failure, of letting the team down, as well as myself. The minimalist style we had chosen for the climb meant we had little leeway. We didn't have metal skyhooks to aid the climb; we would be relying on our fingers and toes. If just one part of the climb proved too tough, we were in trouble; even a 10-foot section of utterly smooth rock could stop us. With food for a week, fixed ropes and a portaledge to sleep on, we could have paced ourselves and rested before each section, but our lightweight approach meant it was all or nothing. It was pure and exhilarating, but the stakes were high.

At the edge of the fjord, in the grey pre-dawn light, I filled our water bottles and then squeezed them into the small ruck-sack. Unimpressed by having to leave his bed so early, his eyelids barely open, Leo tied the ropes on his back.

'These alpine starts are rubbish,' he said groggily.

We worked our way up through boulders and spongy grass, eventually weaving through thickening small trees as the cliff reared up. I thought I had memorised a good route through this impenetrable jungle, but when the trees ended we were faced with blank walls.

'Thought you were a mountain guide,' Leo jibed.

'We need to abseil on to that ledge below us and follow that.'

'Great. I could have had an extra hour in bed.'

He lowered from a small tree, plants all around him, his face a wonderful picture of grumpiness, like a small boy who'd just lost his sweets. I whipped out my camera and snapped. Once down, we crawled unroped along a narrowing strip of vegetation until it ended by a lone tree. Leo tied on and baa-ed like a sheep as I led off up a steepening wall, praying that we were on the right route.

The wall offered cracks and a steep corner above, which fitted with the crumpled diagram I'd stuffed into my back pocket. The rhythm in the movement and the concentration of organising protection relaxed me. Now there was no mental space for worrying about what waited beyond the next few moves. Hanging from the belay above the exquisite steep corner, I stared around at the splendour of the place, and reminded myself of the luck at having chosen this hobby, and not trainspotting, cricket or hockey.

The further we climbed, the more I appreciated the grandeur of the water, azure with white-bleached edges, in itself as impressive as the daggered walls that sliced into it. When we reached the halfway ledge below the difficult upper headwall, it was just after noon, much earlier than anticipated, which both annoyed us and made us happy. If we continued to the top and came across a hard section, we could end up hanging in a horrible uncomfortable position all night, as there were no ledges to speak of between here and the top of the cliff. On the other hand, we had so much time.

'Let's sit it out and chill,' suggested Leo. 'At least we'll be well rested.'

'We do need to be on form tomorrow,' I said, staring upwards.

The wall bent above us as if the gods had tried to pull the

top of the cliff towards the fjord but then abandoned the idea, leaving the upper face warped and overhanging at 15 degrees. On the cracks, I held the kings and queens, but whenever protection became sparse or the holds thinned out, Leo produced the ace. I knew tomorrow we would need all his aces, that mixture of skill and desire; the ability and hunger for uncharted rock where occasionally you had to lie to yourself, pretending things were fine, never thinking about the dark world of blood and broken bones and things much worse.

I realised we were in a special place. A tiny white building nestled down in the depths of the fjord by the water. Limping Joe had maybe lived down there. I wondered if he had been content to return to live here, at the bottom of this chasm; or whether he thought it a prison, and felt bitter that he had never made it to America. My hips ached a bit when I tried to move. One day I would be too old for these things, I realised this now. You couldn't go on for ever, it wasn't like golf. 'Limping Andy', that's what they'd call me.

The Shield had begun as a diversion from climbing in the high mountains, but now it had become all-consuming. And I began to worry again, only this time openly, and Leo surprised me: he was worried too. I liked his openness, the vulnerability, the awareness of the size of the prize versus every possible avenue of failure; the essence of it all. Suddenly, I found myself sounding overly confident, falsely so, only to counter Leo's worries.

Just then a body appeared in the sky, rocketing out above the fjord, followed by a high-pitched strumming. It was probably Adrian, testing his wingsuit.

'Guess what, wise man?'
  'What?'
  'It's your turn to sleep out without a sleeping bag.'
  'I know.'
  'I hope it's not too chilly,' Leo laughed.
  On the left side of the ledge, a shallow cleft butted into the wall. I would squash myself in there, I thought, and escape

any breeze. I tucked my trousers into my socks, put on every item of spare clothing I had and sat on top of an uncoiled rope. I thought of Slingsby and his bivouac during a winter climb in Norway: 'Profiting by experience, for my knees had been cold the first night, I adorned myself for bed as follows, with three pairs of stockings, two pairs of very warm nether garments, trousers and woollen leggings, and then put my feet into the arms of my coat and buttoned it up over my knees; next I had two jerseys, a very thick Islandstroie [Iceland jersey], two shirts, a waistcoat, an overcoat with a hood for my head, a knitted cap over my ears, and warm gloves.'

I was drifting off to sleep, trying not to think of the climb ahead, when a thunderous noise jolted me and I jumped, smacking my head on a protruding rock.

'What the hell was that?' I yelled.

'I threw a big rock off. I'm bored. I'm bored of this ledge.'

'For God's sake, man.'

Leo lit a cigarette that glowed in the low light; I tried to sleep.

At dawn, the wait was over. We could start on The Shield now, hand over to fate, discover what holds geology had made for us. A new day, a new voyage. I massaged my fingers while Leo sipped the tea, his arm resting on his helmet, which still proudly sported the Alfa badge.

I set off, trepidation dissipating as I reached the top of a wide crack. I fixed the belay, signalled for Leo to climb on one rope and pulled up our rucksack on the other. Within a couple of hours we were poised beneath the blankest section of the wall, from below a golden island of featureless rock. Now the protection looked sparse and the holds for the feet and hands poor. Perhaps more importantly, we weren't sure where to go; no one had free-climbed through here before. The first ascentionists had used their skyhooks somewhere, but we might need to go in a different direction. Leo cleaned his boots by spitting on his hands and then rubbing the toes until they squeaked. You needed everything on your side up here.

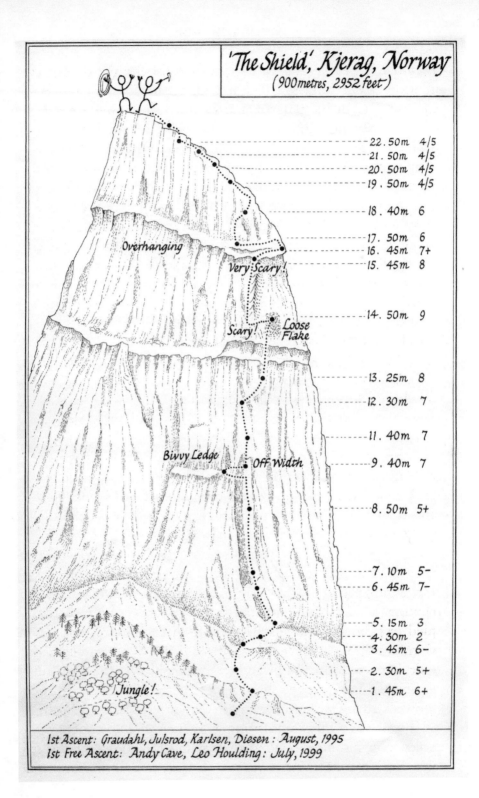

'The Shield', Kjerag, Norway
(900 metres, 2952 feet)

Overhanging

Very Scary!

Scary!   Loose Flake

Bivvy Ledge   Off Width

Jungle!

22. 50m 4/5
21. 50m 4/5
20. 50m 4/5
19. 50m 4/5

18. 40m 6

17. 50m 6
16. 45m 7+
15. 45m 8

14. 50m 9

13. 25m 8
12. 30m 7

11. 40m 7

9. 40m 7

8. 50m 5+

7. 10m 5-
6. 45m 7-

5. 15m 3
4. 30m 2
3. 45m 6-

2. 30m 5+

1. 45m 6+

1st Ascent: Graudahl, Julsrod, Karlsen, Diesen : August, 1995
1st Free Ascent: Andy Cave, Leo Houlding : July, 1999

'Do your best, mate,' I said, wanting to encourage him, but not too much. He was climbing above a series of large, brutally sharp flakes. A big fall here was unthinkable.

After placing some nuts in a crack up above, he moved out on to the wall. He stopped at a good-sized finger edge, the size of a matchbox, and dipped each hand into his chalk bag. He moved on again, fondling holds with his fingers, before moving back to the sanctuary of the matchbox edge, not quite ready to commit himself. He had to unlock a sequence out towards a crack 30 feet away and the hope of more protection. This tactic of advance and retreat gave him more information, but also tired him.

'Right, this is it. Watch me carefully, this looks hard.'

I gripped the ropes tight, shuddering at the thought, the space between us yawning, empty. He began breathing deeply, trying to relax, despite the strain in his arms, despite the terrifying exposure. I wanted to look away but knew I had to watch. Maybe if I was quick enough I could grab a few feet of slack rope and reduce the length of a fall; though the difference between 50 and 55 feet would hardly matter.

Leo reached the crack with his left hand and jumped his right foot up to a small edge, the weight of the hardware around his waist taking its toll. He placed a camming device and exhaled a long, slow growl.

'Good effort, Leo. Take your time,' I shouted across the void, the words vanishing into a brief silence before he clipped the rope through the gate of the karabiner with a crisp snap. He is going to do it, I told myself. He still had tough steep climbing ahead, but he had climbed the section that had occupied our thoughts for days, the section the Norwegians had warned us about. He reached better handholds and climbed quickly up on to a tiny ledge, transferring his body weight on to his feet. Hanging from one arm, he rested his cheek against the wall, shaking the other arm, trying to bring it back to life.

Having watched Leo carefully and having chalk on the handholds, plus a rope above my head, made my job of following this section much easier; nevertheless, it was hard climbing and I felt my forearms swelling as soon as my fingers left the matchbox edge. I wouldn't die if I fell off, but I would end up dangling in space and we would lose a lot of precious time.

'Very impressive, Leo. I don't think I could have led that,' I said respectfully when I pulled up on to his belay ledge.

His display of commitment, of pushing on into the unknown, had inspired me. Now it was my turn to open the way and take control. I glanced up at the intermittent crack that charged up the stupidly overhanging wall. This is it, I thought. Something in my chest swelled, a power, a self-belief. Down in the fjord, over 2000 feet below, a yacht cruised in the calm water; it looked like a child's toy. We took a drink from the water bottle and nibbled on a cereal bar.

I set off, applying just the right amount of pressure through my fingers. You had to grip, but if you gripped too hard you would tire in seconds and fall. I blasted up the crack, but halfway it closed. I stuck my foot up high, threw my right hand out into the base of a new crack. The protection was much better than what Leo had found on his pitch.

'This is crazy,' I laughed, enjoying myself.

The rock had beautiful scallops shaped into it, like large grey tears. Some of these gave positive edges for my fingers, which allowed me to recover and shake my arms out. Towards the top I tired, but the endorphins were pumping now. I was in a trance. At last, after climbing about 160 feet, I reached a small foot ledge and got the weight off my arms for the first time. We were up near the top of the Shield feature now.

'I think we've cracked this baby,' I hollered, passing the rope through my belay karabiner.

'Nice work, Cavey!' Leo yelled up. He looked so alone, way below, strapped to the middle of the wall. 'This is an un-believable climb, man. The rock is made for free-climbing,' he said as he approached me, the spare rope hanging out in space.

Leo had climbed on some of the world's greatest big cliffs, so it was indeed some endorsement. The climb weaved through such ludicrously steep terrain. One day, I thought, it would rank as one of the great traditional free climbs of Europe. I pulled out the scrap of paper with the route description.

'The aid route goes out right now, on loose rock apparently.'

'This should be the last hard section.'

The realisation of the dream was tantalisingly close now.

Leo climbed up to a curious hole, arranged protection, and then traversed carefully out to the very right-hand edge of the wall. When I reached the hole he began shouting: 'Check the flower out, Andy. Smell the flower.'

Somehow a lone white buddleia had taken root here. Adjusting my feet on the tiny holds, I leaned in and sniffed at the petals, soft against my nose. The sweet scent lingered in my nostrils as I now looked rightwards, realising the seriousness of the ground ahead. The colour of the rock had darkened and many of the holds felt hollow and creaked as I pulled on them.

'Lovely flower, Leo, but how the hell do you do this next section?' I yelled.

'Get your hands on that big loose flake and traverse. It's not hard, just a bit scary.'

Leo hadn't placed much protection, probably because of the loose rock, which meant that if I fell I would pendulum into space and fly past his stance on the arête. I had got cold on the belay, but now my face and my armpits felt clammy. The thought of a flake tearing from the wall and slicing through the rope flashed through my mind.

'Check out the inversion, Andy,' Leo said as I arrived at the arête, relieved to have made it safely. Sun-tinged clouds, like candy floss, had flooded the fjord. I had been so stressed I hadn't seen the spectacle.

We climbed for another 300 feet up awkward walls and grooves until the angle began to ease. We had hardly eaten or drunk anything for hours now, our feet were sore and both my hands were swollen.

'This isn't climbing. This is boring; it's like walking,' complained Leo.

'We'll be there soon. Calm down.' He hasn't had a smoke for a while, that's why he's agitated, I thought.

'I hate this sort of crap.'

The cliff started to lean back so that we were almost walking. On top we shook tired, torn hands, a big moon rising behind us. We had free-climbed The Shield and it felt wonderful.

A small man appeared, walking across the grass towards us.

'*Bonsoir*,' he said and continued to the edge of the cliff.

He held a radio that suddenly crackled to life.

'Hi, this is Tracey. What's going on up there?'

'I will come now.'

'There's a lot of cloud down here, man, I'm not sure it's a smart idea.'

The man walked to the very edge of the cliff, raised his arms and leapt into space.

We sat on our rucksacks on platform three at Doncaster railway station, the ghetto-blaster, complete with fresh batteries, between us, pumping out dance tunes. Next to us a large group of middle-aged women sipped lager. They were returning from a hen weekend and hadn't quite finished the celebrations.

'So do you reckon you'll take up base jumping?' I asked Leo.

'It looks so cool, I'd love to have a go. Can you imagine climbing a massive route and then flying off?'

'It would save all the effort of descending, that's for sure.'

'I wonder if anybody has ever soloed a big route wearing a chute on their backs.'

'What do you mean?'

'That could be the ultimate. You could climb at your limit on some really steep big wall and then, if you blew it and fell, you could just fly.'

'Are you serious?'

'Can you imagine it?'

By now the women were dancing to the music and asking Leo to get up and join them. He declined, but clapped his hands in appreciation of their antics. A cleaner appeared out of the gents' toilet with a bucket and mop. The largest of the women took the mop from him and told her friends to hold it while she began limbo dancing under it.

'I would like to try base jumping once,' I said, as the train approached.

'You couldn't do something like that once. You'd want more of it.'

8

Eiger of the Yukon

The late summer wind wrestled leaves from the trees down to the ground, the grass bleached from weeks of sun. Gathering recruits for the exodus, a flock of birds flashed across the sky like a fast, twisting black kite. Between the neat white walls, the car rolled up and down the corrugated land, past Hucklow and Foolow towards plague village Eyam. I opened the window and, feeling the air on my face, thought about what mountains meant to me.

Over the years, mountaineering had become my portal to strange, empty, often unspoilt places. I loved the departure from the routine of everyday life, the feeling of having sprouted new eyes with which to view the world afresh. These adventures in the mountains made the world feel large again. I enjoyed the unpredictable nature of life on a journey into the greater ranges, and I loved the problem-solving, especially the task of unlocking a mountain's secret, of finding a way to the summit via an untrodden path. The rock-climbing trip to Norway had been fun, but in my heart I hankered for those higher, emptier places. Some people interpret travelling in such wild landscapes as a thirst for solitude, a quest for loneliness; perhaps they are right.

I still felt anxious about the commitment needed to complete a multi-day route in the high mountains. Sometimes fear flooded in too. Nevertheless, I had arranged to spend the evening with Mick Fowler, climbing, and then chatting over a pint about the possibility of an expedition together the following spring.

I turned along the dale until I was below the tall white cliffs of Stoney Middleton and parked up. I fastened the rope to my rucksack as a huge truck rumbled past, the noise of clashing metal from its undercarriage bouncing off the cliffs, a taste of dust lingering in the air. Local legend records that in 1762 a girl named Hannah Baddeley jumped from the cliff edge opposite, attempting to end her life after being abandoned by her lover. It is said that her billowing petticoats contributed to her survival. It was vertical for over 100 feet, and, having seen countless base jumpers plummet off cliffs in Norway earlier in the year, I just couldn't believe the story, even if she had landed in a tree.

Mick arrived just then, with his rosy cheeks and unmistakable beaming smile.

'Andrew, it's a great pleasure to see you again,' he said, holding out his hand, his banter as eccentric as ever.

He switched his weight from one foot to the other, visibly excited about the prospect of rock-climbing, and changed quickly from his tax inspector's shirt into his climbing clothes. We walked along the dusty road and then darted into the woods and up on to Windy Ledge, the rock golden in the late sun. We waved at some of Mick's friends who were already climbing.

'The question is, Andrew, where to go? Bearing in mind I only have three weeks' leave officially, four at a push.'

'Quick access and low altitude, I guess. Greenland? Patagonia? Baffin Island? Alaska?' I said, uncoiling the rope.

'Yes, I'd never thought of Alaska before,' Mick replied pensively. 'I've always enjoyed the cultural ethnic action of India and Pakistan. North America is similar to Britain, I would imagine.'

'Two countries separated by a common language. A short trip would suit me,' I said.

Mick tied into the rope and set off up the wall. The climbing was reasonable but the holds were as smooth as glass. Mick had a relaxed style and moved up full of confidence. These days he is known for his bold exploits at altitude, but over the years he has also established countless terrifying rock climbs. At the time, due to work and family commitments, he climbed on rock sporadically, preferring to accrue enough free time to make an expedition to the higher mountains. Since our débâcle on Changabang in 1997, he had attempted a desperate new route on Siula Chico in Peru with Simon Yates, but they had turned back due to dangerous conditions. Earlier this year, though, Mick and Steve Sustad had succeeded on the first ascent of the Arwa Tower in India; a typically lightweight, bold approach had paid off.

'Time for another pitch, Mick?' I said.

'Absolutely.'

The trip to Norway had left me fit and confident. I eyed up Circe, a classic steep climb with an exhilarating finish requiring exacting footwork and a cool head. I'd done it before some years ago, but it would still be a test.

I felt the hunger to try it despite a suddenly darkening sky and the threat of rain.

'It's too overhanging to get wet anyhow,' joked Mick.

I remembered the tiny hold and then the skip an inch higher into the small, slippery pocket. Below, on the road, cars rushed by, commuters heading home. I clipped the rope through a long piton and headed out horizontally along the roof, feeling the pressure. A local builder, Tom Proctor, had first climbed this in 1977. I wondered whether he'd inherited strength genes from the years of lead and then flour spa mining in the dale. All his routes were brutally physical, and every picture I'd seen of him showed abnormally large biceps and shoulders. At the end of the traverse, the drizzle had begun to settle on my glasses. I quickly jumped with my hand to a distant but positive hold and rocked over, elated, knowing I had cracked it.

'Proficiently ascended, Andrew,' hollered Mick from below.

'Thank you, Michael,' I replied, trying not to laugh.

I moved cautiously over dust-covered sloping holds that

soaked up the rain. I felt light and invincible and forgot about the world as I crawled over the top. Having passed the rope through a sling attached to a tree, Mick lowered me to the ground.

'Proctor did all these lines years ago, way ahead of the time,' I said, untying from the rope.

'It was a good era,' Mick said, grinning.

He had moved to Sheffield at that time to dedicate himself to climbing full-time, but after a year, bored by the somewhat parochial climbing scene, he returned to London. Encouraged by his father, he looked for 'a proper job' and started work with the Inland Revenue, remaining a civil servant ever since. His razor-sharp mind, annoying organisation and ability to seek out the positive from a situation, no matter how difficult, had helped him reach the upper echelons of the tax office.

Mick followed the climb, taking out the equipment, but then with much of the rock damp from the rain, we packed up our gear and headed towards the pub, shouting our plans to the others. I stopped off for chips. Mick went direct to the bar; he could survive on beer and crisps no problem. Outside, by the river, I devoured the food and remembered how I'd first met Mick through Joe Simpson. Joe was one of the first climbers I ever met in Sheffield. Steve, a friend from Doncaster, and I had slept out below Lawrencefield quarry and woke covered in an inch of wet snow. We were hitchhiking up on the main road, shivering, when a Renault 4 painted in large black and white checks pulled over.

'Where are you going?' asked the driver, a small man wearing a trilby, with a very posh voice.

'Grindleford café, mister, please.'

'Of course, hop in.'

'You a climber?' I asked.

'Yes, but not on days like this. It's foul out there.'

When we pulled up at the café, we thanked him profusely.

'Not a problem. By the way, what are you doing this evening?'

'Nowt, why?'

'Well, there's a party in Sheffield. Come along if you like, Gatefield Road. Folk will meet in the Broadfield beforehand.'

'What's your name?'

'Joe, Joe Simpson.'

'I'm Andy, and this is Steve.'

Intrigued, if slightly nervous, we went along that evening and witnessed dyed hair, mohicans, Joy Division and The Smiths.

'If you ever need somewhere to stay,' Joe said, in the middle of the night, 'here's my number. I live with John Stephenson, that guy over there.'

The following year I stayed at their house on a few occasions and enjoyed their company immensely. Joe's leg was in a terrible mess following his epic on Siula Grande in Peru. One time I stayed up all night reading the unpublished manuscript of his book, *Touching the Void*. Another evening, Mick Fowler arrived and slept over. We went to the pub, and after several beers he organised a competition to see who could stick the most matches up their nostrils by placing them one at a time between the teeth and then using only the tongue to hoick them up. On the journey home he challenged me to climb up an enormous drainpipe. I set off, not stopping until I got to the top to peer down. To my horror, Mick had been replaced by an irate policeman. I slid down, unaware of how pink my top lip and nostrils were from the silly match game. After rollicking me, the policeman let me go.

The following year, Joe invited me on a trip to the Karakorum to try an unclimbed peak. Coincidentally, Simon Yates asked me on a separate expedition, also in the Karakorum. I accepted both, as the suggested dates fitted perfectly. The day before flying out to Pakistan, I celebrated my twenty-first birthday with a monumental party here at Stoney Middleton. I remember waking up with a raging hangover and finding a beer mat on the bedside table. On it was scrawled, 'Meet us at the Golden Peak Inn, Gilgit, 23 July, Cheers, Simon (Yates).' The great British explorers Tilman and Shipton had always reckoned that, ideally, an expedition could be planned on the back of an envelope. I felt a beer mat was one step further. Unfortunately, debilitated by my hangover, I managed to miss my flight and had to wait a further three days before I could leave for Pakistan.

It was strange to think that here I was again, twelve years on, entering the exact same pub thinking about heading off to the big mountains. It was comforting, if a little peculiar, how life went full circle sometimes. So much had happened in the intervening years. Nowadays I knew how cruel the mountains could be; perhaps I'd traded this for innocence.

Inside, Mick licked his lips, eager for us to decide on a venue.

'I need something to dream of when I'm sat at the tax desk,' he said. 'Another trip to Siula Chico in Peru might be a possibility.'

'I thought you said it was a death trap?'

'Well, if we went earlier in the year it might be colder and safer.'

'It sounded horrible, giant blocks whizzing past your head.'

'El Niño, Andy, global warming, that's what Simon reckons.'

'It sounds grim to me.' I paused: 'It must have been freaky for Simon. I mean, being back there, where he and Joe had their epic.'

'I saw where Joe crawled. I couldn't believe it. It's absolutely miles, horrific, totally horrific.'

I shuddered and shook my head before lifting my pint. 'What about Alaska? The Moose's Tooth, Mount Dickey, Mount Hunter?' I began.

'Paul is always raving about Alaska.'

'It's a big world out there, Mick.'

'And so little time,' Mick said, before swilling the last of his pint. 'It's a worry, Andrew.'

Over the next few weeks, we put our minds to finding an inspiring objective. Mick's close friend Paul Ramsden convinced him that Alaska provided unlimited adventure with many unclimbed technical lines remaining and achievable in four weeks, providing the weather treated you kindly. Paul himself was considering returning the following year with a team to attempt a peak named Mount Kennedy.

When Mick emailed the renowned American alpinist Mark Twight and asked him about good unclimbed lines in North America, he received a boisterous reply. Twight, a leading exponent of bold technical alpinism, regularly wrote passionate pieces about the ideals of modern mountaineering, sometimes causing offence. I knew of him through Andy Parkin; the pair had climbed some magnificent new routes together in the Alps. He encouraged us to come and test our skills and our luck, but warned us of the weather.

Rumour has it you want a good ass-kicking in Alaska (the best bang for the buck in the world in my opinion, but flights from the lower 48 are cheap for us).

It ain't easy coming up with striking new projects in the region, it's totally climbed out and you shouldn't bother to go poking around up there – a waste of time.

Hah! Perhaps the Yanks are reluctant to divulge the gems which remain.

Mt Kennedy north face awaits an Alpine-style ascent. Then again, the seracs bordering the face are not as benign as one might hope.

Most hard routes in Alaska are condition-dependent (true everywhere, I suppose), so beware . . . some guys get lucky their first time out; others spend a lot of time and money before tasting a morsel of success. How lucky do you feel?

I'm not much help, but no one else seemed willing to say a word – except to steer you in a sad direction. We joked an awful lot about it too. Let's send them to . . .

Anyway, good luck. Perhaps we'll see you up there.
Mark F. Twight

I suppose that after Changabang and the Patagonia trip, I felt I deserved some luck, but I knew better than to believe that the mountain gods paid out according to what you thought you were owed.

A couple of weeks later I received photographs of peaks in the St Elias Mountains from Mick. One of the images stood out above all the others. It had been taken on a beautiful freezing February afternoon in 1935 by the American photographer and mountaineer Bradford Washburn as part of a National Geographic Society-sponsored exploratory Yukon expedition. The pilot of a single-engine ski plane had flown up the Kaskawulsh Glacier towards an area labelled on the map as 'unexplored mountains and glaciers'. They'd ventured into the heart of this totally blank area of almost 5000 square miles, a land previously unseen by man. Suddenly, between two rounded icy peaks rose a sharp, Himalayan-looking mountain of immense grandeur 'flanked with staggering precipices of ice and granite'. Washburn wrote that after many 'long flights, and even after months of ground exploration, this new peak stood out vividly as the most exciting and majestic of the scores we discovered. I have kept a photographic enlargement of the mountain before my desk for many years. To me it epitomised all the mighty mountain grandeur of Alaska and the Yukon.'

Now I stared at the same photo, and though it was only a photocopy, I could feel myself falling under the mountain's spell. It looked perfectly symmetrical, an elegant ridge falling directly from the summit down to the glacier; a huge arrowhead of ice and rock aiming at the sky, one half lit, the other in darkness. It was an easy mountain to fall in love with. Beneath the image it read 'Mt Kennedy (4238m) from the north, Bradford Washburn collection'.

One evening the following month, Elaine and I travelled over the hill to our friends Brian and Louise Hall's house for dinner. Louise, who had once owned a highly successful restaurant, always served up wonderful food, and Brian had agreed to show me photographs from a recent trip to the St Elias Mountains where he had been in charge of safety during the making of a documentary film about steep skiing.

'It really is an incredible place,' Brian began. He was a

powerfully built Lakeland man with a gentle smile. 'Although the summit heights are modest compared to the Himalayas, it feels like a serious place.'

'You can access these mountains quickly with helicopters or aeroplanes, I suppose.'

'Yes, in theory, but you get such prolonged periods of bad weather, and the pilots only like to fly when it's good. I'll show you some photos after we've eaten.'

I had first met Brian in Chamonix where he and Louise used to live, running a chalet and a guiding business. He had encouraged me to become a mountain guide and subsequently employed me. Brian had been one of the first British mountain guides to set up home in the Alps. During the 1970s and 80s he had formed part of a small group of elite British alpinists who pushed the limits of what was possible in mountaineering. Following success in the Alps and then South America, he and his friends moved on to the Himalayas, making bold, fast, alpine-style ascents of Jannu and Nuptse, as well as attempting Everest during winter. Sadly, during the early 1980s a high number of Brian's friends lost their lives. The deaths of Alex McIntyre, Peter Boardman, Joe Tasker and then Alan Rouse — all in the Himalayas — took their toll. His close companion and fellow mountain guide Roger Baxter-Jones was also killed in an accident whilst guiding in Chamonix.

'You know, Andy, the Himalayas just stopped being fun any more,' Brian said.

I understood perfectly. Losing Brendan on Changabang had shocked me. I wasn't sure I would ever recover fully, but I did want to try and return. With each fatality, it became more and more difficult to sell yourself the myth that you could evade catastrophe. Sure, often there was an error of judgement rather than fate, yet making errors at great altitudes happens even to the best, it seems.

Brian had a deep love and respect for nature and he was a talented photographer. He also had a passion for film, and in recent years he has made a career of it, establishing and running a company that specialises in logistics and safety for films shooting in remote or hazardous locations. Now he projected a beautiful photograph of a seemingly endless mountain range on to the wall.

'The St Elias Mountains: it's a phenomenal place. I mean, if something went wrong in there it would be serious,' he remarked.

'What do you mean?'

'Well, in the Himalayas, normally if you travel for a day or so, eventually you reach local people who might be able to help. But here, once the pilot drops you off, that's it, you are totally on your own.'

'What's the weather like?'

'Ah, well.' Brian started laughing, a deep-chested, rattling laugh. 'When we were there it snowed a hell of a lot. In fact I witnessed one of the biggest avalanches I've ever seen, almost a kilometre wide. Utterly terrifying. Fortunately, we were on this spur over here.' He pointed to a ridge on a snowy mountain.

'Windslab avalanche?'

'Probably.'

'And what about objectives? What are the challenges there?'

The next photograph showed a stunning pyramidal mountain of steep rock and ice reminiscent of the Eiger north face in Switzerland. I recognised it; it was Mount Kennedy.

'I don't think it has ever been climbed in alpine style, though lots of people have tried. Alex Lowe, Jack Tackle, et cetera. Allegedly it's one of *the* things to do over there.'

'Those guys are awesome mountaineers. What's the catch?'

'The weather, I suppose. And the size of it. This north face is nearly eighteen hundred metres from the glacier to the summit.'

'Where do the pilots land?'

'You would have to contact them. We were given the name of two: Andy Williams in Whitehorse and a guy called Kurt Gloyer over in Yakutat.'

After exhaustive research, Mick proclaimed the north face of Mount Kennedy to be, in his view, the most impressive objective, certainly in the St Elias range. What was more, Paul Ramsden and friends had decided to visit elsewhere. We received an encouraging email from American climber Jack Tackle too. He and Jack Roberts had climbed high on the face before treacherous storms had forced them back. Lower down, Tackle had accidentally dropped a crampon, and the pair had continued up as best they could with Roberts doing the leading. Their line followed a series of ice runnels that cut through impressive steep granite walls. It was exactly the sort of thing Mick and I were looking for, and we decided that our primary objective would be to complete this route to the summit.

Bradford Washburn had suggested the peak to the National Geographic, which in 1964 had been asked to recommend a prominent mountain that could be named in honour of the assassinated president, John F. Kennedy. The following year, the president's brother, Bobby Kennedy, was flown by heli-copter to the upper slopes of the mountain to a waiting team of America's most experienced mountain guides and a prepared snow cave. The guides reconnoitred the route to within a couple of hundred feet of the summit. The following day Bobby and the guides made the first ascent via a straightforward snow route. It was a five-day round trip for the Senator.

Over the next few days, I found myself thinking about the peak more often, sometimes with joy, but at other times with dread. It was a jewel of a mountain. Mick's ardent enthusiasm helped counter the fear I felt periodically about returning to serious mountaineering.

'Kennedy looks stunning,' I told Mick. 'But it's much bigger than I thought.'

'It's giving me the urge, Andy,' Mick said.

'And it sounds really remote.'

'I was thinking of asking another two people to come, just from a safety point of view.'

'Seems sensible,' I said.

'We have to pray the weather is on our side. Incidentally, I just found out that Geoff Hornby went to the same area recently.'

'And?'

'Thirteen feet of snow fell in twelve days. They hardly left the tent.'

Thirteen feet of snow: I couldn't get the words out of my mind. That night, before getting into bed, I stood on my tiptoes and reached to the ceiling. That was about eight feet, I pondered. I shook my head in disbelief. I would need to get out climbing in Scotland over the winter, I thought. Do something decent and hard.

9

Genesis

A large pair of eyes sparkled briefly before the stag leapt across the icy road, antlers flashing like the crown of an Arctic prince. Dave held the wheel without flinching and the animal vanished into deep snow and the night. Earlier, in Edinburgh, the bright February moon had hung just above the horizon. Now it sat higher, casting the still shadows of small crofts across the silver land. It was the sort of night you lay awake in bed, dreaming.

'Have you ever been to Kishorn?' I said.

'Never heard of it.'

'It's a beautiful loch, a bit further on, totally unspoilt-looking.'

'Sounds nice.'

'The amazing thing is, during the seventies and eighties, more than two thousand men worked there, constructing oil platforms. Nowadays there's no sign whatsoever of any industry. It's as if the whole thing never really happened.'

'Presumably it's a deep loch, that's why they used it.'

'Exactly,' I said. 'Walt Thompson from Glencoe, he worked there.'

The movement of people on and off this land stretched back in time, small, scattered traces of other worlds. What you thought was wild and untamed space had in fact felt the hand of man. People stayed in a place for different reasons. The wildness for some fulfilled a deep spiritual and cultural need, an ancient connection to the land, as well as a modest living. For others, it was something to be endured, for maximum gain in the economic game. Men jockeying for position; callous, selfish, abusive. Further down Loch Kishorn sits a line of white cottages, originally built to house crofters evicted during the Highland Clearances.

'What a stunning evening.'

'Nowhere better when it's like this.'

Over the years, my feelings for the Scottish hills had become deeper, a wave of emotion that kept growing. I had always loved the mountains here, but now, after years of travelling to faraway ranges, I understood their true significance, especially here on the west coast, especially in winter.

'At the conference in Edinburgh, one guy talked about memory and identity,' I said. 'He looked at how people with Scottish ancestry living in America imagine the place. These are people who have never been to Scotland.'

'And?'

'It seems that many of the mental maps they hold are what they've gleaned from tourist brochures and websites, all the clichés: lochs, heather, distilleries. He even had some statistic about thousands of people living in New York who've bought heather originating from Scotland by mail and then planted it in window boxes outside their apartments.'

'It's a mad world.'

I had enjoyed the conference. Afterwards a few of us had walked from the School of Scottish Studies over to the Sandy Bells. I sunk a pint, listening to a couple of fiddlers and a woman with a beautiful voice. I sipped at the second pint and listened to the others bemoaning the lack of funding in the humanities. I couldn't relax and started to fidget. The big moon, the falling temperatures; I drifted off, dreaming of what could be out in the mountains. I visualised the unclimbed line of ice and turf, a line I had tried before, imagining it to be perfectly formed. It had got a grip of my mind.

I excused myself, feeling awkward and knowing that I was sacrificing a fun evening, but I had arranged to meet Dave on the other side of the city at 8 p.m. We would drive up to the north-west in my car and I would then drop him off in Stirling early on Sunday evening so that he could get a lift back south with some friends. I had to be back up north as I was guiding in the Cairngorms the following week.

'So how many times have you tried this climb already?' Dave asked.

'Twice really, though I've never actually set off up it; it's never been in good condition.'

'What's it like?'

'It climbs out of a huge cave then follows a fault line. When you see it, you'll want to do it. It was thawing the first time we looked at it.'

'Then you tried it again?'

'The second time was even more pathetic. We arrived at a bed and breakfast in Lochcarron at half eleven at night, and the owner came out in a T-shirt. The forecast was all wrong, it suddenly got really warm in the night and then started to rain. It was a complete waste of time.'

'Third time lucky, Andy.'

One of the main challenges of climbing in Scotland during winter is finding good conditions. The frequent fluctuations in temperature, especially on the west coast, allow unique 'plastic ice' to form over the rocks. Wet snow plastered on to steep walls by strong winds and existing melting snow can suddenly freeze if the temperature drops sufficiently. Mountains such as Beinn Bhàn, which sit so close to the sea, are particularly vulnerable to rises in temperature; an increase of just a few degrees can result in the ice quickly disappearing. A Scottish winter climb can bud, flower and die in the course of a single day. Trying to climb here can be extremely frustrating, and yet somehow its fickle nature is what makes it so special.

It is never easy unearthing great new winter climbs in Scotland. Understandably, local climbers become precious about significant 'last great problems' and, living close by, they are much better placed to judge conditions. Nevertheless, over the years we had sneaked up and snatched a few prize ascents. The defeat in Patagonia the previous year still rankled in our minds. It would be great to do something good together, something new and hard. You needed patience, skill, local knowledge and luck in abundance to succeed on climbs like the one we were heading for.

The ludicrous Bealach na Ba road climbs up to 550 metres above sea level, twisting and exposed like a road in the Dolomites. At the top, we parked the car and curled up in our sleeping bags on the ground. It was freezing cold, the moon had disappeared and the sky was crammed with glinting stars.

'It's two o'clock now, I think we should get up at four,' Dave said. 'A bit of breakfast and then set off. What do you reckon?'

'Sounds fine,' I lied, glancing up at the stars before my eyelids closed tight. The last time we'd slept out in the mountains together was in Patagonia.

A couple of hours later we stared at the map by head torch. It looked around five kilometres of relatively even ground to the col between Sgurr a' Chaorachain and Beinn Bhàn. Just north of there, a slope looked to lead us steeply down into Coire nan Fhamhair. I set the compass to follow the course of a stalker's path, though it was buried under a metre of well-frozen snow. We walked in silence, our light beams rocking in time, the stillness interrupted only by the gentle crunching of our boots on the concrete snow. Dawn crept up on us, a slow glide into daylight. We stopped and turned off our head torches, sipped some water, smooth sandstone boulders standing above us, ancient, perfect somehow. The further we walked, the more I forgot about things: academia, the unpaid bills, the disturbing stories I'd read in newspapers, the world. At the cliff edge I peered over and the sight of the steep walls took my breath away. The legend Andy Nisbet had summed it up, calling it 'a colossal evil face' with 'breathtaking exposure' and adding for good measure an 'absence of obvious lines' with 'limited protection' and 'suspect belays'. It always looks worse from above, I tried to reassure myself.

'Amazing,' Dave said, full of excitement, as we descended beneath the 800-foot ice-smattered dark wall of Nisbet's 'Der Riesenwand'.

Alone beneath one of the most dramatically steep winter walls in Scotland, I thought: these are the moments that make a climber's life. Neither of us had a camera; it didn't matter. I felt it inside: timeless, enduring beauty. A light so special and tender that it stunned you and you almost forgot why you were here, that you had vertical things to perform. Then I remembered Paul Nunn turning to me one gorgeous day just as the cliffs of Creag Meagaidh were being lit by the sun, and saying: 'Do you know, Andy, if I can get out for a walk in my old age and see this, I'll be satisfied. It would be enough.'

Dave passed me a cereal bar. It made me sad that Paul had not made it to those gentler days. I remembered how he had encouraged us to explore beyond the regular haunts of Glencoe and Ben Nevis, as magnificent as they are. 'Drive a bit further, you won't be disappointed with what you find.'

And here we were. We put on our harnesses and crampons and moved across the steepening slope, an ice axe just for balance. We didn't speak much, wanting to leave the gods alone, not wanting to boast about how good the conditions were until we had actually seen evidence with our own eyes that the climb existed. But as we rounded the corrie and I saw the intermittent line of ice in the back of the cave, I couldn't help myself.

'You beauty!' I bellowed.

'Is it that massive chasm on the left?'

'Dave, my friend, it's our lucky day.'

At the bottom we stared blankly. There appeared to be no way up the lower part of the cave. Curiously, footprints led to the base of the climb and then back out, though it didn't look as if anyone had been any higher.

'I can't see how we're going to start it, Dave. The upper

part of the climb looks crazy, but possible at least. Here, it looks impossible.'

'Let's have a look, you never know. It does look ludicrous, though. But amazing, utterly amazing.'

'I always spot the lines; doesn't mean I can do them, of course.'

I stood on my tiptoes and swung at icicles that hung like dragon's teeth from the wall of the cave. Reluctant to accept the pick of my ice axe, they shattered and tumbled over my shoulder, sounding like smashing glass, before thudding into the snow by my feet. If only, I thought, if only I could get it to stick. Before long I had ripped the whole lot down. I retreated to the floor of the cave, walked over the shattered icicles, dejected. The huge gulf between dream and reality. Three attempts, 3000 miles of driving, packing bags, unpacking bags, organising gear, coiling ropes, phoning partners, checking the weather four times a day, it never ended. And when you finally found it frozen, still it wasn't enough.

'Bollocks,' I cursed.

I had got hot thrashing around and took off the hat from under my helmet. I was drying the sweat from my forehead when I spotted it. To my left, a small shelf ran out and up towards a steep wall daubed with small islands of ice. I put my helmet back on and traversed out left.

'Watch me, Dave. I'm going to have a look out here.'

I sidestepped along the ledge, nose against the wall. Before long it was so narrow I had no alternative but to crouch down. I rested on my hands and knees, my right hip and shoulder against the rock, my backside towards Dave. I crawled along the increasingly narrow strip of snowy turf on all fours, like a lost sheep. When the ledge ended I hooked my ice axe into a small crack in the rock above my head and pulled myself up.

'You won't find that technique in any winter climbing manuals!'

'Excellent,' Dave shouted up.

Thrilled with the absurdity of the crawling technique, I set off up the wall, moving from one island of ice to another. How whimsical a climber's spirit is, I thought, as with each passing move I felt buoyed inside. If Dave could make it up the thinly iced wall above, we would have circumnavigated the steep lower part of the chimney and gained the main fault line.

'Certainly different,' Dave commented when he arrived at the belay.

He moved up the wall piercing small patches of turf and ice with his axes, a committed, determined look about him. I felt as if all the frustration and disappointment of our Patagonian climb was being channelled into this new adventure. His crampons danced on the wall, lost for a while, scratching like hungry, desperate mice until they bit on small edges of rock. He paused, placed a small wire in a crack, clipped the rope. He took a deep breath and then set off again.

'Keep going, Dave. Looks like there's a corner soon and some protection.'

'It's OK,' he muttered. 'It's OK.'

Dave always gave the impression he could stay in a strenuous position for ever if he had to. He climbed methodically and calmly for 100 feet and then pulled up on to a decent ledge. He cleared snow from the rocks, searching for a place to secure the ropes.

'Safe,' he shouted down eventually, the words bouncing from the sides of the cave. I enjoyed the intricate climbing with the security of the rope above my head. I moved freely, without pressure, enjoying the game, making minor adjustments that improved my balance and lessened the strain on my arms. I traversed right along a ramp of turf, the wall beneath undercut, giving sensational exposure.

'Looks tasty above,' Dave said when I reached him.

I peered at the fragile ice smear that ran up and out of view to the left. This will be the test, I thought. This is a line that has to be crossed, or not. I could hand over to Dave if it looked too dangerous.

'Belay good?'

'It's really good, Andy.'

'OK, keep an eye on me, this looks desperate.'

I moved my shoulders, tried to warm them a bit and then worked up towards the ice. I felt my heart thump faster as I got established on the measly thin ice. I wished I had a description from a climbing guidebook that might help, or someone else's advice – 'just keep going and it will get good again' – anything in which to put my faith, but when I peered up all I saw was more of the same. The unknown. Fragile slivers of ice, half-promises. I placed an ice screw, but the teeth hit rock after just two inches. I tied it off and clipped in the rope. Wouldn't hang my school bag off that, I muttered. And yet the act of placing it had briefly taken my mind off where I was and what I had got into. I moved precariously up to the steepest part of the ice. It was like climbing on the side walls of a broken wine glass. I tried to moderate my breathing, prayed that the ice would stay attached to the rock, for a little longer at least. In my mind the rope ceased to be of any use; it sagged towards Dave, worthless. A fall from here and only darkness beckoned. The longest sleep. The end.

Without warning the ice supporting my left foot collapsed. I stabbed my foot against the rock that remained, but it started quivering. I had to move somewhere, fast. This urgency gave me calm, a certainty within the chaos, control over the fear. I plunged my ice axe and tore a tuft of turf from the base of a corner, smelt a whiff of earth and then swung again, the pick biting in the frozen dirt. I balanced the points of my crampons on a pencil-thin edge and rested my shoulder against the rock. I stared down, the blackness of the cave, all its disgusting evilness, sucking at my arms. I was tiring, but I was too good for it, I felt it in my heart. I threw my leg up and rocked my weight on to a small ledge. I rested my head against the wall, a delayed surge of adrenalin racing in my arms, my heart thumping like a small angry fist.

I stared at the green of the moss and the clear veneers of water dribbles, frozen on to the wall. Miniature works of art, here today, gone tomorrow. I arranged the belay slowly, drained.

When Dave arrived he gave me a look, a silent nod of the head. I had travelled very close to darkness and survived. To give a nod like that you had to have felt fear yourself, the metallic taste, the dry throat.

'The weather's changing,' said Dave.

I looked up. Snowflakes filled the air, and higher still I could hear the wind. He plucked the remaining equipment from my harness, organised it, methodically clipping it on to his own harness.

'That groove looks like the best option,' I said. 'You should get some decent protection.'

'It's quite a sustained route, isn't it?'

'Feels like it to me.'

'We can't be that far from where the angle eases. Another pitch maybe?'

'Don't speak too soon.'

He laughed and then hooked both his ice axes into the base of the steep rock groove. It looked awkward, but he kept calm, placing protection and climbing steadily.

By the time I joined him I had numb fingers and a deep hunger; we'd eaten very little all day. The slope leading to the summit plateau had collected a surprising amount of fresh snow. You couldn't relax on terrain like this. We remained roped together, placing occasional pieces of protection as snow started to cascade down. On the top we shook hands; it was too wild for words.

After our shared frustration in Patagonia, it felt great to finish such a major climb. The euphoria was difficult to describe, but impossible to replace. To succeed on routes like this, you had to take risks. We could have gone to Ben Nevis and done one of the classic hard routes we had heard was in condition, but instead we had dared to take a chance here. We could have abseiled down the climb and checked for gear, or even climbed it first in summer, so as to lessen the unknown. But we wanted more than that; we desired the unknown. We wanted a rigorous test; we wanted the raw, undiluted challenge. It was pure and simple.

We hadn't seen another soul all day, and the complexity and seriousness of the climbing, combined with the mesmerising beauty of the place, had revived me. For the first time in a long while, I felt alive again. The numbness was fading and the joy returning. We took off our crampons, put the ropes away, ate a small cereal bar each and then set the compass.

Our feet rested on top of the snow for the first few paces, but then we both crashed through simultaneously up to our knees. 'Argh!' I yelled into the wind that came with all its fury across the sea through the forest of Applecross, accelerating along the snow, becoming angrier still until meeting Beinn Bhàn, the highest thing in its path, and us. It wasn't cold; in fact that was the problem: the wind had warmed the snow, loosening the bonds between the particles, meaning our feet punched through. We fought to lift our thighs out of the drenched white mush, then lost our balance in the wind and stumbled again. The rain stung my face and pounded the hood of my jacket like small stones. Alaska with Mick won't be any worse than this, I told myself.

10

North

Sometimes the world feels tiny. You travel to the other side of the globe on holiday and meet a man from your home town. 'It's a small world,' you joke, slightly disappointed by the dilution of the idea that to travel far is to find distance from your everyday life. 'The world is a handkerchief,' the Spanish would say. Your imagination desired and believed in a place without the inevitable reminder of home. It is less a desire for loneliness and more a longing for a unique encounter, a selfish adventure.

More than anything else, the invention of the aeroplane has made the world a smaller place. Like the television, this piece of engineering changed the course of history for millions of people, changed our view of the world, changed the size of our world. I didn't imagine that we would meet many people we knew up in the Yukon, but still, I appreciated that without the invention of the aeroplane we probably wouldn't have planned to climb there. In fact, without the aeroplane, Mount Kennedy, our mountain, would have remained undiscovered for much longer.

The more I read, the more I realised that Bradford Washburn, director of Boston's Museum of Science, was the one who had opened up the interior of the St Elias Mountains in the Yukon. His stunning black-and-white aerial images of peaks and glaciers had inspired generations of mountaineers, and continue to do so. Roping himself and his enormous large-format camera – weighing over 50lb – into the open cargo doorway of the aircraft, he photographed previously unseen peaks. Afterwards he processed the film with chemicals and makeshift equipment in tents down on the glacier. Washburn was also an expert cartographer, and during these exploratory flights through the St Elias, he sketched details of the glaciers on to the blank sections of the existing maps: his maps of Mount McKinley, Mount Everest and the Grand Canyon remain state of the art. As a mountaineer he climbed eight first ascents in North America, his trip with Bob Bates to Mount Luciana right in the heart of the St Elias perhaps the most renowned.

Washburn knew from his exploration and surveying in 1935 that Mount Luciana, at 5226 metres, remained the highest unclimbed peak in North America. The chief difficulty was its overwhelming remoteness. He knew better than anyone that the best way to reach such a mountain was by aeroplane, but the problem was that most pilots refused to fly anywhere near the vast, eerie St Elias Mountains. The thought of landing a plane on a glacier there was totally unthinkable. On the advice of friends, in 1936 Washburn wrote to a pilot in Valdez named Bob Reeve, a man who had a growing reputation for skilful, adventurous mountain flying. Reeve's reply was short and to the point: 'ANYWHERE YOU'LL RIDE I'LL FLY.' A delighted young Washburn began organising his two-man expedition for the coming July.

Something of a restless kid from a small town in Wisconsin, Reeve's first experience of flying was with a couple of barn-stormers in Texas, appropriately named Hazard and Maverick. In 1928, following a brief spell in the Army Air Force, he took a job flying in South America for the United States Post Office. The enthusiasm for flying down there delighted him. The necessity of air travel due to the mountainous terrain meant that the public were much more willing to accept the risks than in North America. Like Franco Bianco, who flew with

Agostini in the extreme south, and Antoine Saint-Exupéry, Reeve was a true pioneer, who could adapt to the ever-changing conditions that mountain flying presented, someone who learnt quickly. One technique the mail pilots developed to minimise the risks of flying in the daily thunderstorms and violent winds of the Argentinian pampas involved flying just a few feet off the ground. However, this disturbed the cattle, and on one occasion an irate gaucho shot and damaged Reeve's friend's plane, so they stopped that tactic.

A few years later Reeve made his way to Alaska, eventually settling in Valdez. He had been reckless with the money he had earned in South America and needed to start again from scratch. He offered to repair a damaged plane for a local pilot and then began hiring it out. It was the post-Klondike years and many places were downbeat, though the hopeful pioneering spirit remained among some miners. Reeve saw a gap in the market and began flying prospectors to remote and difficult locations. He started making landings on glaciers using skis, the bases lined with metal from a counter taken from a saloon bar. His antics, particularly short takeoffs and landings, began attracting attention from established pilots such as Harold Gillam, who commented: 'I thought Reeve was 90 per cent pilot and 10 per cent nuts. But now I know damn well he's 10 per cent pilot and 90 per cent nuts!' Perhaps revelling in his own mythology, Reeve had painted on the side of his tool shed in Valdez, 'Always use Reeve Airways, slow unreliable unfair crooked scared unlicensed and nuts.'

During the long flight in towards Mount Luciana, Reeve, who always chain-smoked, leaned towards Bradford Washburn and shouted over the noise of the engine, 'That cloud bank ahead is too low. We have ten minutes more before we'll have too little gas to get home. What do you think?'

'Anywhere you'll fly, we'll ride,' replied Washburn.

Reeve powered on, eventually landing his single-engine Fairchild on the Walsh Glacier at an altitude of 8750 feet, setting a world record for the highest landing ever made by a loaded plane. Unfortunately, warm summer temperatures had destroyed the fabric of the snow and on landing the plane's skis sank under the surface, making it impossible for Reeve to take off again. Reeve began to worry, as to walk out from there would take days and he was inadequately equipped. He was not a mountaineer and dreaded the idea of crevasses.

'I'm a pilot, not a mountain-climber. You skin your skunks and I'll skin mine,' he growled to the two young mountaineers as they wearily moved around the crevassed glacier, digging out the plane.

They spent three days digging and sitting out foul weather. Finally Reeve decided to try and escape. The two climbers watched open-mouthed, partly in horror, partly in admiration. As Reeve himself recalled to his biographer, Beth Day: 'I gave it the gun and off I went. But by God, I hadn't gone a hundred feet when smack! Down into a crevasse. But I wasn't stopping. The engine was developing tremendous power, far beyond its rated capability. I climbed right out of the crevasse and kept going. Then flop! Down into another – and I lost the air speed I'd gained, getting out of it. Bumpety bump, it was just like driving over a plowed road. I realized I was getting nowhere. I'd already run a mile or more, and ahead of me I could see the big crevasses – wide enough to hold a boxcar. If I hit them I was a goner. Then I happened to glance left and spotted an icefall, sheering off the side – maybe a 250 feet drop. It was my last chance. I made a sharp left turn and dove the plane right over that icefall. It mushed straight for the bottom, and I thought maybe I was a goner, after all. But the plane had achieved just enough forward speed on the jump-over to become airborne. I levelled out about ten feet from the bottom. That was the greatest feeling of my life – bar none!'

Bates and Washburn shrieked for joy.

The two men went on to reach the summit of Luciana, before making a committing seven-day journey out via the Donjek Glacier to Kluane Lake. It was a superb achievement done in lightweight style. The men acknowledged the vital importance of Reeve to their success and Washburn later claimed Reeve as being 'without doubt the finest ski pilot and rough country flyer I have ever seen'.

We were planning to visit during May and so hopefully wouldn't have the issue of the plane sinking into slushy snow. I volunteered to enquire about mountain pilots and travel arrangements generally. I rang a friend, Andy Broom, who had helped guide a party up Mount Logan the previous year.

'You either fly in from the Canadian side, from Vancouver up to Whitehorse, or from Seattle in the States up to a town called Yakutat. We flew from Yakutat with a guy called Kurt Gloyer.'

'Someone else has mentioned him,' I said.

'Kurt is very good at getting you close to your objective and he has a good reputation for getting you back out on time. He's also a great bloke.'

'What's Yakutat like?'

'It's a tiny place but the people are friendly. Kurt knows everyone; you'll end up going for a few beers with him, no doubt.'

'Sounds like he's the man.'

'He's a damn good pilot,' Andy said.

'It doesn't get any easier saying goodbye to the family,' Mick said as the jet taxied down the runway at Birmingham airport. 'Last night my daughter Tess asked, "Daddy, why are you leaving us to go off and climb a mountain?"'

'What did you say?'

'It's desperate, she's ten and Alex is seven. Basically, I said that many people do nothing with their lives and that I get great satisfaction and pride from going to remote parts of the world and climbing mountains. I am doing something with my life.'

'What did she make of that?'

'It's hard, but hopefully I'll return a happy man,' he said, smiling candidly. 'What about Elaine?'

'She's amazing really. She doesn't say much, maybe she hides it.'

'She climbs so she understands, I suppose?'

'Her dad was a committed mountaineer and the rest of the family are mad on the outdoors. She's really got into the mountains since meeting me, though.'

'My wife approves of me climbing with you.'

'What do you mean?' I said, as the plane became airborne.

'I think Nicky thinks that because you're married and you are a mountain guide, you're safe.'

'I'm pretty cautious, that's what I tell myself anyhow.'

'To be honest, in the future I can imagine doing more shorter trips, like this one. Hey, did I tell you, the Mount Everest Foundation wrote to us again? They've given us a grant of thirteen hundred pounds.'

'Great.'

'But they've also questioned our plan to be away for only three weeks. They don't believe it's long enough for a route like the north face of Kennedy. The St Elias is renowned for appalling weather, I suppose.'

It would be a coup if we pulled it off. Particularly as so many strong teams had failed.

At Chicago airport, rather bored at waiting for the connecting flight to Seattle, Mick started moving around taking photographs of the obese specimens that waddled up and down the polished stone aisles.

'Just trying to capture some of the Chicago bum, Andrew,' he laughed as we searched for somewhere to eat.

I was mesmerised by the number of giant people, but I was too shy to photograph them. I had a few fat friends, but this was of a different order.

'I wouldn't want to be tied to him if he fell in a crevasse,' I said, pointing to one man, his buttocks the size of car wheels and wobbling like jelly.

Initially, Mick had worried that this trip would not include enough cultural and ethnic interest, but as he strained over a seat clutching his camera in wide-angle mode, he appeared more than satisfied. And we were nowhere near Alaska yet. The fun ended abruptly, however, when we tried to board our flight to Seattle and experienced the American phenomenon of airlines overbooking their flights.

'Sorry, gentlemen, this flight is full.'

'Excuse me, we are booked on to this flight,' said Mick, waving his boarding card.

'I am sorry, sir, this flight is full now.'

Mick went quiet, his face assuming a grave look. The British are famous for their ability to stand in queues and for not complaining about things, but this was different. Mick's time is precious, and to maximise it he is ruthlessly organised. Something had just stepped in the way of his plans and he was furious.

'Can I speak to the manager, please?'

'Excuse me, sir, I do apologise.'

The next time Mick spoke, he raised his voice, something I had never witnessed before. I stood back.

'I said can I speak to the manager, this is outrageous. We booked these flights months ago.'

Mick applied the same tenacious approach to the predicament as if trying to climb a steep, thinly iced wall. Much to our disgust, we were promised some monetary compensation for the inconvenience and seats on the next flight.

We sat for four hours, our interest in Chicago's finest washed away with endless cups of coffee. As we started to board the plane, we heard a shout.

'What the hell are Cave and Fowler doing here?'

Turning, we saw Duncan Tunstall striding towards us, with Chris Pasteur in tow. Duncan and Chris, the other half of our expedition, had flown via London on a much later flight, and we had not been due to meet them until Seattle. Still seething over the airline's incompetence, Mick explained what had happened.

I had known Duncan for years, on and off. Energetic, with broad shoulders and thick black curly hair, he commiserated with us loudly. Chris was bigger, but more reserved, with short sandy hair and a beard.

'We'll catch you later,' he said softly as we shuffled past the desk.

When we finally arrived in Seattle, we took a taxi to the north side of the city where Ade Miller lived. Ade was an acquaintance of Mick's via the Alpine Club in London. I shook his hand and then collapsed into a chair.

'Better go shopping, I suppose,' Mick said.

I looked at my watch. I couldn't fathom how long we had been travelling but it felt like a lifetime. Exhausted, I felt as if someone was pushing needles into my eyeballs. 'Couldn't we do the shopping tomorrow morning?' I suggested.

'We'd lose a day if we did that,' Mick said persuasively. 'We have a pretty early flight up to Yakutat.'

I didn't trust him to do the shopping alone. I remembered the weekend on the Isle of Skye in winter, where he seemed content eating a few slices of bread and margarine and the odd bag of crisps. The memories of Brendan and me running out of food on Changabang were fresh in my mind too. I wanted to eat well, and if the weather remained poor and we were stranded out on the glacier, we would need plenty of food.

Seattle has a history of being a jumping-off point for ambitious people heading to the Yukon. On 17 June 1897, 60 miners arrived there on the steamship *Portland* from the Yukon with gold worth over $800,000. At that time, the economy was difficult and uncertain. People became hysterical reading the headlines, and Seattle newspapers had an interest in the hype as it bolstered the city's claim to be *the* place to collect supplies before going north. The journalist Tappan Adney noted: 'The news that the telegraph is bringing the past few days of the wonderful things of Klondike, in the land of the midnight sun, has opened the floodgates, and a stream of humanity is pouring through Seattle and on to the golden mecca to the north.'

Within days all available boats were full, with one in ten people being turned away. Traders capitalised, selling clothing, food and other provisions to the eager, often naïve prospectors. In Victoria, British Columbia, Adney gathered his own supplies for the trip north. 'Those best qualified to express an opinion say that there is nothing better than a deer skin coat with a hood – an Eskimo garment called a parka. Then one should have a fur robe . . . In the order of preference Arctic hare is first. Next is white rabbit, the skins being cut into strips, then plaited and sewed together. One needs nothing else in the coldest weather, although one can thrust one's fingers through it. Both rabbit and hare robes are scarce and last only a year. Lynx, fox, wolf, marmot make good robes, bear is almost too heavy for travelling. I was fortunate indeed to pick up even a marmot-skin robe, eight feet long and five wide, lined with a blanket, Indian-made, from somewhere up the coast.'

Towards the end of July, the *Times* in London warned of the dangers of departing in summer, as it meant people would have to endure the long Arctic winter. But the tide was too great to turn. The Canadian historian Pierre Berton claimed that, of the 100,000 people who set out to reach the Klondike in 1897–99, only about one third actually arrived. Only half of those went on to work in the gold fields and only a few hundred actually got rich. Most who made fortunes managed to squander them on booze or poor investments before they made it back south.

In the Seattle supermarket, anyone looking at our trolley might have thought that we were heading off for a couple of months' gold-prospecting. I bought a whole leg of cured ham, slabs of cheese, tins of fish. Before leaving the UK, I had met with a dietitian who had expressed concern over our meagre intake of food on these punishing multiday climbs. In particular she highlighted the lack of protein in our diet, pointing out that without it, the body begins to break down and performance is compromised enormously. The problem was how to carry the food, bearing in mind proteins such as salami, tuna and beans are relatively heavy items. Having something that didn't require heating up would be useful. She suggested nuts as a source of protein, and so I loaded a giant bag of cashews on to the top of the heaped trolley.

'Wow, that looks like a lot of food, Andy,' said Mick, suddenly appearing from the adjacent aisle.

'This is just our half; Chris and Duncan are in the next aisle with their own trolley,' I said. 'Could you look for some Parmesan; a couple of blocks should do it.'

'Are you serious?'

'I like eating,' I responded laconically. 'Imagine if we have four metres of snow like Geoff Hornby, or the pilot can't get back in? We'll be glad of it then.'

'I take your point, but still . . .'

'Trust me on this one. It's not like we can pop down to the shop once we're there.'

I stared past the checkout boy through the glass and into the dark of the street beyond, my eyes stinging. I looked forward to arriving at base camp so that I could get a decent night's sleep.

The following morning I woke up on another aeroplane, disorientated. Mick was staring out of the window. I glanced over his shoulder through one eye. Jagged rock peaks rose from the ocean, stretching towards the horizon, the lower slopes smothered in forests and occasionally cut by dark chasms.

'It's outrageous out here. For the last hour there hasn't been any sign of habitation and it looks wild, cliffs everywhere,' Mick said.

Suddenly, a much bigger wall of rock rose out of the ocean at a distinctive kink in the coastline, and what looked to be a collection of islands. Mick began photographing it and then moved aside so I could get a better look. It looked enormous, though it was difficult to judge how high exactly.

'I wonder where that is,' said Mick.

'It might be south of a place called Prince Rupert,' I said, staring at a map in the seat pocket. In a while we would fly out of Canada into a narrow coastal strip of America known as the Alaskan Panhandle. 'But it could be anywhere,' I added drowsily.

An air hostess approached serving tea and coffee, smiling more sincerely than was usual.

'Excuse me,' Mick said. 'Could you tell me where we are at the moment, please?'

'Sure, now let me see,' she said, locking her trolley. Leaning over some empty seats, she gazed out of the window for a few moments.

'Canada, sir, I'm pretty certain that's Canada,' she laughed, shrugging her shoulders.

I suppose she had a point. Although dramatic, it all started to look the same after a while. This was wildness on a scale not known in Europe. It was an empty land, savage and inhospitable. Such a landscape would be difficult to travel over by foot, the sort of place you could easily vanish without trace. A speck of dust in a desert. If a plane faltered here, Lord knows how you'd survive.

Afterwards, looking at a more detailed map, I realised that we had been close to the town of Ketchikan, the scene of a tragic plane crash back in January 1943. Ignoring warnings of severe storms, the legendary pioneering pilot Harold Gillam decided to make the normally routine flight from Seattle to Alaska with five passengers. Four hours into the journey he hit terrific turbulence. The only radio call he made was to say, 'I'm in trouble' and 'One engine is out.' The plane plunged 4000 feet, narrowly missed a mountainside and eventually hit a tree before diving into the snow. Forty military and civilian planes scoured the coastal mountains, and coast guards searched the coast for a fortnight before the search was abandoned. Because Gillam had not used his radio until the end, no one knew where the crash had occurred. A month after the disappearance, a patrol boat spotted smoke on a beach and then saw two crazed bearded men screaming and waving. The crew took them for insane lost trappers, but they were in fact survivors of the crash. Two more men were found higher up in a freezing hut. The survivors were so emaciated and frostbitten that it brought the rescuers to tears. Gillam was still missing, and the fifth passenger, a young woman, had died from serious injuries within 48 hours of the crash. Gillam was eventually found further away. With severe injuries he had climbed up a hill and attempted to light a fire so as to attract attention. He had been dead for several weeks.

As our plane began its descent into Juneau, the capital of Alaska, I struck up conversation with the man opposite.

'Impressive scenery out there. Supposed to be good skiing in this town.'

'When it snows here no one goes to work, dude. That's how good the skiing is.'

'Lots of powder, yes?'

'Oh boy, like you couldn't imagine. I've lived all over the States and I'm telling you, buddy, on the right day this is paradise.'

'You live here?'

'Sure.'

'Have you just been off somewhere?'

'I had an interview for a job down in LA. Then I went east to visit family, just a real quick hit.'

He wiped his nose. 'You guys on vacation from England, right?'

'Yes, we're climbers, heading up to the St Elias Mountains.'

'Oh really, that will be a serious adventure.'

The willingness of some Americans to travel always surprised me. They moved around at such a pace, without thinking twice, fragments of their lives spread far and wide, a relative here, a job there. When Elaine and I had moved 14 miles from the centre of Sheffield, some friends had questioned how we were going to cope 'out in the sticks'. Of course there are plenty of Americans who never leave their home state; only a quarter of Americans own a passport.

As the jet lost height, a range of snow-covered peaks filled the windows on one side, islands and small harbours on the other. An Alaskan jet had crashed earlier in the year and everyone on board had been killed, but this didn't worry me as much as I thought it would; in a sense, you had handed over control to the pilots and there was absolutely nothing you could do about it.

We were allowed to get off for an hour and a half at Juneau. The surrounding scenery was magnificent, and right outside the airport a line of small planes floated on a long channel of water, a sort of aqua runway. I felt sad that we wouldn't have more time here, but recognised that that was the price of having a firm objective to focus on. You rushed all the way to the mountain and then afterwards you were exhausted and just wanted to get home.

In the airport terminal, a huge stuffed polar bear stood on its rear legs inside a glass box. Its teeth and claws looked particularly menacing. Mick stood next to it and I snapped him with my camera.

'Not nearly as big or impressive as the specimens we saw at Chicago airport,' I joked.

'A lot of these guys are going fishing and hunting,' said Duncan, pointing to the other passengers waiting to get back on the plane. I turned around. It was all checked shirts, beards and baseball caps. There were no other mountaineer-looking types, despite the fact that the plane went all the way to Anchorage, the jump-off spot for Denali, the highest peak in North America. 'They seemed a bit confused when I told them we were going climbing,' he added.

Alaska had always been a place people visited to collect valuable materials: fur, fish, gold and more recently oil. Hunting on the land, for residents and visitors, was very much part of the culture. You sensed that mountain-climbing was a sideshow up here, a peculiar and rather pointless activity with no material gain.

Back on the plane, Mick handed me an article that highlighted the wildness of the area. The St Elias had almost 40 virgin summits over 3600 metres high; a dozen of these were over 4000 metres, and one, Mount Atlantic, was the same height as Mont Blanc. Twenty-four of the peaks had been climbed only once. Most ascents, by far, were of the normal route on Mount Logan (5951 metres), the highest summit in the range

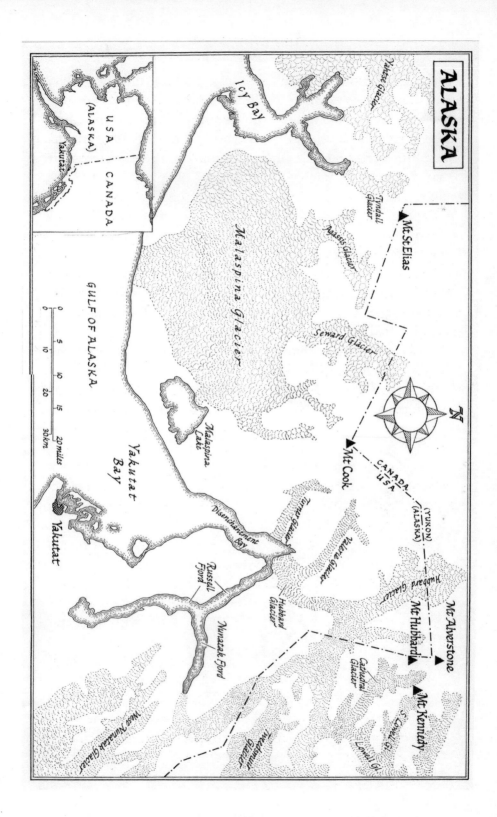

and the biggest mountain mass in the world, measuring 169 miles around its perimeter. Until recently Mount Logan had received on average around one ascent per year since its first ascent in 1925. Nowadays, a busy year in the St Elias Mountains might mean 70 people. Hardly a motorway, when you consider that during the summer, hundreds of people can reach the summit of Mont Blanc each day.

As the jet approached Yakutat, I wondered what the trip ahead held in store for us. Personally, I knew that my resolve would be tested and I'd find out if I still had the head and the heart for it, but at least I was climbing with Mick. I had total belief in him. On Changabang I had seen him under immense pressure. Only then, when everything has been stripped bare, do you see the core of someone. You couldn't see this in a café or a bar; you needed to observe someone in the raging wind and with hunger, then you saw how the light reflected off them. In India, I'd seen Mick Fowler as bare as a man could ever be, and I knew that he could be called upon if needed.

11

Flight

The most impressive thing at the airport was an ice cliff on the edge of the runway. Snow cleared through the winter and spring had been piled into a steep-sided mound, and now the lump the size of a hotel looked solid and frozen, in no hurry to melt. If our pilot reckons we can't fly in for a while, we can amuse ourselves climbing up and down that, I thought. We headed towards the modest airport building; a dog limped slowly past, and behind us a vulture scowled down from a wooden post.

In July 1805, Captain Yuri Lisianski, an Imperial Russian Navy Commander, made the first recorded mountain climb in Alaska. The previous year, Lisianski had helped Governor Baranov recapture Mikhailovsk, the capital of Russian America, from the Tlingit Indians, thereby regaining control over fur trade activities. Mount Edgecumbe, a 976-metre extinct volcano by Sitka Sound, had been named by James Cook during his voyage up the north-west coast in the late 1700s. Some historians have speculated that the ascent aimed to display rule over the local region.

Russians wanted local sea otter pelts, considered the finest fur in the world, and when stocks ran low around their bases in the Aleutian Islands, they began searching along the south-east coast, the area inhabited by the Tlingit. The Tlingit, however, refused to be conquered and continued to wage war on the Russians well into the 1850s. After all, the Russians were relative newcomers.

For those with time and money, by the 1880s Alaska had become a tourist destination. Harold Topham, a member of the Alpine Club in London and an extremely strong mountaineer, led a four-man expedition to Mount St Elias in 1888. From Sitka it took seven days by sea just to reach Yakutat. Topham's party was unimpressed with both the boat and the skipper; the boat smelled of seal blubber and constantly veered towards the rocky coast, and when they finally made it to Yakutat, the skipper ran aground on a reef 300 yards from shore. Topham wasn't impressed with the Tlingit Indians either, and his account of the expedition bears all the hallmarks of the prejudice peculiar to that time. He wrote: 'Provided a government gunboat has been along the coast shortly before your visit, the people will be friendly; if it has not, you had better keep away.'

The Indians obviously felt it was an occasion having these well-dressed 'King George men' visit their isolated village, so much so that they decided to delay their annual sea otter fishing trip. Topham had taken a couple of porters from Sitka, but needed more to help carry equipment up to the foot of the mountain. He arranged to meet the chief, who donned his best clothes for the event. As Topham describes: 'He had on an evening dress waistcoat and trousers, and a naval cap; and he stood, surrounded by his dirty family, at the foot of some feather mattresses on which he requested us to be seated. He was much more interested in our clothes than answering our questions about canoes and men ... he made us promise ... to give, upon our return, so many of our clothes that we should have been reduced to a state of nature ...'

At least one of the Indians had worked as a porter before, for Seton Karr's expedition two years earlier. The 10 Indians that Topham hired didn't appear keen to depart immediately. Topham protested and the Indians reluctantly loaded the expedition's two tonnes of equipment into canoes and set out across the ocean. After just one hour, they claimed a ferocious storm was imminent and so the party duly returned. When the weather remained clear and the Indians announced that they would be attending a feast that evening in the village, Topham was furious, commenting that 'the weather always is bad if the Indians wish it to be so'. In a lecture to the members of the Alpine Club back in London, he explained that 'an Indian won't be hurried' and although they 'will carry 70 or 80 pounds a day over rough ground, they cannot climb'.

It had taken the Topham expedition weeks just to travel to Yakutat with their equipment. We had got here at midday, the day after leaving Britain. Many passengers had stayed on board the plane destined for Anchorage. Adjacent to the runway, half a dozen small planes were parked outside an aircraft hangar; straight ahead there was a fuel station, and in the left corner a place to eat. Yakutat is the least populated place in North America to be serviced by a scheduled daily flight. The village has one bank, one taxi, no roads out and a population of around 600. It isn't a place at which you stop off out of curiosity. People come here for a reason.

'Welcome to Yakutat,' Kurt said, shaking all of our hands in turn. He was a slightly built man, quietly spoken, with an easy manner.

'How's the weather looking?' asked Mick.

'You guys sure got lucky,' Kurt replied, hooking his thumbs into the pockets of his faded blue jeans. 'The weather has been awful for over a week and today is the first clear day; we should fly this afternoon, you never know what tomorrow will bring.'

'What, like straight away?' asked Duncan.

'In a couple hours maybe. I need to show you guys a video, kind of park regulations stuff, and get you to fill in a couple of forms.' He smiled, rubbing his index finger against his moustache and then tugging down his baseball cap. In a crowd Kurt appeared unobtrusive, a shy man.

'Excellent news,' said Mick.

'So would we have been struggling to fly in last week?' asked Chris.

'Oh boy, it's been damn miserable. You would have been sitting right here for days.'

We moved our bags to the Gulf Air Taxi hangar by the edge of the runway opposite the ice mound, an aircraft hangar-cum-workshop, with a small office attached. Outside sat a small red-and-white Cessna equipped with skis; presumably this was our plane. Kurt then drove us to his house in a rusting, unkempt Datsun, which reminded me of the cars back home in the 1970s.

'Do you get many climbers visiting these parts?'

'Some, Logan usually, but fishing is the big thing, and hunting. Last few years the surfers have been coming too.'

'That sounds masochistic,' I said.

'I believe it's pretty chilly, but they reckon it's world class.'

'The fishing is awesome here, boys, so if we can get the summit knocked off sharpish, we could hire a boat. What do you reckon?' said Duncan.

'I fished on the local canal once for about half an hour,' I said. 'I'm not sure I've got the patience.'

'We're not talking two-pound perch here, Cavey, with your flat cap and flask,' said Duncan.

I couldn't imagine Mick sitting still long enough for fishing. He fidgeted the whole time. Come to think of it, I couldn't imagine Duncan fishing either. His brain worked overtime and I found it hard to keep track of his garrulous speech. In fairness, less than 48 hours ago he'd been buying and selling millions of pounds' worth of oil, and I reckoned it would take him a while to relax; not that the pace of the expedition had been very relaxing so far. By contrast, Chris, a civil engineer, spoke occasionally and always with a gentle thoughtfulness. The pair had met at university in Durham and started mountaineering together. They were clearly very fond of each other and had a solid climbing partnership.

As he drove, Kurt waved to every vehicle that passed.

'Everyone must know everybody in a place like this,' I said.

'Oh, that was my ex-wife's family.'

'Does she still live here?'

'No, she lives over in Haines with my daughters,' he said.

'Is that far?' asked Chris.

'Not so far to fly. It would be a good walk, though,' Kurt laughed.

'I can't imagine this road goes very far,' I said.

'This road is twelve miles long,' he said.

Graced by few roads, Alaska relies on small aircraft. There are reportedly about 10,000 small planes and 9500 active pilots, or one for every 58 residents. In 1997, a fairly typical year, the Federal Aviation Administration recorded 162 small plane accidents with 51 fatalities. As one visitor calculated, that meant the odds of a pilot being involved in an accident were one in 61, only slightly better than the chance of an American soldier being wounded in Vietnam. You are twice as likely to be killed as a pilot in Alaska than in commercial fishing. What did that make the business of Alaskan mountain flying?

As we drove along, we could see the frailty of the place. A few scattered buildings hidden in the trees by the side of the road. A small harbour, a haven on the long coast where surf pounded the glaciers flowing into the sea. Dots of civilisation, on the edge of a vast land. Small green shoots by a frozen desert.

Kurt started the official Kluane National Park video, a warning about the dangers out there and how we should organise ourselves. I sensed he understood we were fairly experienced, and he seemed almost embarrassed having to make us endure such a formality. We sipped coffee to stay awake, our bodies sinking further into the settee. Most of the video consisted of common-sense points, but it alerted us to how wild the place was. It wasn't so much the glaciers and the mountains; we were used to that. It was more the river crossings and the wildlife, primarily the grizzly bears.

'You guys eat fish?' hollered Kurt from the kitchen. 'I got some you can take with you if you want.'

'Sounds great,' said Chris. 'Fish curry at base camp.'

Kurt appeared with two enormous bags, one full of halibut, the other crammed with giant prawns.

'I gotta make room in the freezer. There's so much fish in there right now; some guy gave me a load more last week, a gang I'd flown in.'

'Hey, Kurt, how common is it to see a bear around here?' I asked.

'Well, not so long ago I heard a noise out there on the porch. When I went out to look, lo and behold there was this bear.'

'Big?'

'It was a grizzly, about eight feet tall.'

'Christ, that sounds terrifying.'

'I couldn't lock the door quick enough, but it's very unusual to have them come to the house.'

'We should have brought the pepper sprays Paul Ramsden recommended,' said Mick.

Just before leaving, Paul had recounted an alarming story of a long trek he had made alone in the north of Alaska. Walking through dense woodland, days from civilisation, he stumbled upon a family of grizzlies. Before leaving, he had been sold an emergency bear attack device consisting of a strap around the chest which housed a pressurised canister of pepper. The idea, he explained, was to wait until the attacking bear was very close to you and then try to aim the pepper into its face. These enormous aggressive animals hate pepper, and if all goes to plan they should run away. Fortunately, Paul managed to pass without needing to use his ammunition.

'I need to give you these too,' Kurt said, handing us a couple of radios the size of small house bricks. 'Park regulations. If you have any problems, you can call in to the office here or to the park.'

Back at the Gulf Air office, we sorted through our equipment, ensuring key items would be to hand once we landed on the glacier.

I put my big boots on.

'The weather could be grim up there; we should keep the tent handy,' I said.

The truth was, we had never flown into a base camp before and weren't quite sure what to expect. Normally, during the walk-in, you have plenty of time to chat with each other, relax and prepare gradually for the mammoth task ahead. On this occasion, if all went well, in a couple of hours we would be sitting on the glacier below the north face of Mount Kennedy, having had no time whatsoever to adjust to the mountain environment. It felt like we had been travelling for an age, but on planes and in airports and supermarkets.

We went up to the hotel for a pint and a burger. Whereas bars in Zermatt, Yosemite, Glencoe or even Kathmandu often decorate their walls with climbing paraphernalia for the benefit of visitors, here it was all fishing and hunting. Antlers nailed to the wall, photos of fishermen dwarfed by halibut weighing 300lb, and signs recommending the lodges' guides, experts in hunting 'brown bear [grizzly], glacier bear and mountain goat'. 'Each room has its own freezer,' boasted the literature. I tried to visualise putting a dead grizzly into a freezer, but then realised it wasn't necessary, as lodge staff would willingly 'prepare any trophies for shipment to your favourite taxidermist'. On account of the good weather and the fact that we were flying straight into the mountains, we would contribute very little to the local economy compared to the hunters and fishermen.

The impressive runway at Yakutat was built during World War II for military aircraft en route to the offensive with the Japanese further north. Despite the grandeur of the runway, there were no people on the tarmac telling you where you could and couldn't walk, and there were to be no on-board lectures from Kurt about what to do in the case of an emergency. No tea or coffee on a flight like this, no perfume sales. I climbed into the back of the Cessna surrounded by ropes, tents and food, and tightened the safety belt around my waist. Mick sat in the front. When Kurt climbed in, I noticed that the only extra clothes he had brought for the trip were a pair of blue nylon gaiters and a jacket.

Kurt put on his headphones, gesticulating to us to don ours too. The noise of the engine starting set my heart racing: the purr and growl of air and fuel exploding. As a teenager I had owned numerous motorbikes and I had always loved the sound of their engines, each with a unique resonance. The three blades of the propeller spinning faster and faster soon became a slicing blur, adding another layer of sound. We taxied out towards the centre of the runway. Many boys start out loving steam trains, I theorised, some flirt with motorbikes, but I am convinced all dream of flying in machines like this one day. In theory we had been flying in aeroplanes over the past two days, but now I realised that we may as well have been sitting on a coach. Here, a few millimetres of fragile glass and the fabric of the plane's thin body was all that was between me and the world. And we were going to land on a glacier. I started to laugh, but quickly tightened my stomach and screwed my fists, trying to control the giddiness. The thought came again: we were going to land on a glacier in this: essentially a Mini Clubman that someone had stuck tiny wings and a propeller to.

Kurt braked the plane, increased the revs and then let it off the leash. I stared out of the side window and watched the greenery of the trees whizz by. As we became airborne, climbing away from the ground, the engine sounded less aggressive but still loud. Kurt flicked a switch and on came Bob Dylan, the master of the ballad, revealing the fate of Hurricane.

Down below, square forests shrank as we climbed higher. I hoped to see a bear, but we were already too high. Then a long rainbow spread below us and I took a photo just before the plane swayed in the air. I glanced at the dashboard through the gap between Kurt and Mick's shoulders, hoping to see our speed. There were so many different dials and gauges I gave up. We flew over lakes and rivers so numerous that many remain nameless. The forests disappeared first, then the rivers began to freeze: brief black floes of ice that soon vanished beneath snow. All that remained were hints of where rivers might be in summer, slight shadows in the white. Wire-thin veins. The enormous Malaspina Glacier then filled the window on the left. Outside of the polar regions, it is the biggest glacial mass in the world, three times the size of Greater London. I suddenly appreciated why it had taken eight expeditions before Mount St Elias was climbed.

We crossed an enormous lake. Kurt released the retractable hydraulic skis, a manoeuvre just audible over the engine and the music. This radical invention by Maury King allowed climbers to be set down by plane right in the middle of these mountains, without the costs of a huge pack train. I stared around. Just to get back from this point would take days on the ground, yet we had been in the air less than 10 minutes. It was both exhilarating and terrifying to witness such a vast landscape, a place unknown to me. The St Elias Mountains are 200 miles long, and in terms of vertical relief, from the ocean to the summits they exceed the Himalayas. The further we travelled, the larger the world felt.

Experts speculate that the earliest settlers to Alaska came across the Bering land bridge at least 10,000 years ago, perhaps earlier. Those that located to the south-east of the St Elias Mountains, around Yakutat Bay, formed part of the Tlingit tribe that Harold Topham had encountered. A hunter-gatherer, coast-based group, they had developed a unique and rich culture as a direct result of the tremendous natural resources available in the area. What in other parts of the world people had to fashion out of the ground by cultivation, here nature provided. With vegetables and game on the land and the ocean rich with salmon, halibut, cod and herring as well as sea lions and whales, the Tlingit had more time than others to devote to leisure, cere-mony and protecting their territory.

They built spirit houses, where the ashes from cremated dead relatives would be placed, and used 'owned words', status-assigned language, spoken during formal encounters. Tlingit people placed an importance on the supernatural when fishing, gambling or waging war. The practice of *potlatch* is perhaps the most difficult for outsiders to fathom. The ceremony entailed host individuals enhancing their reputation and validating their social rank by giving away useful items, such as storable food, canoes or even slaves, to his own or neighbouring tribesmen, often to the impoverishment of himself. Many, such as the early missionaries, interpreted the event and its accompanying feasting and dancing as a terrible waste, and even satanic, which led to it being banned by the Canadian and American governments in the late nineteenth century.

The Tlingit took land ownership extremely seriously, allowing no one to hunt on their land without an agreement. Coastal Tlingits negotiated rights with neighbouring clans to travel east of the mountains in winter in order to dry berries and fish away from the damp coast air. Visiting gold miners were allowed to kill beaver for food but were obliged to give the skins to local Indians. In 1847, Serebrennikov and his entire party from the Russian-American Company were killed by the Ahtna tribe while trying to explore the interior of the Copper River area just to the north. Overhunting by the Russians had vastly reduced the fur population, and growing interest in the area from the British and Americans added further pressure to the Russian enterprise. Eventually, in 1867, Russian America was sold to the USA for $7.2 million, much to the disgust of the Tlingit and other native groups, who never accepted that it was the Russians' land to sell.

Kurt beat his thumb against the denim of his right knee in time with Dylan. I wondered what he was thinking about. I knew virtually nothing about the man, but he seemed very content up here. It was a mad, dangerous job and a hard way to make a few dollars, but you sensed that for Kurt, this was more than a job. Normally, the people who assisted us in reaching the mountain stopped at the edge of steepness: the yak herders of Tibet, the porters of India or Pakistan, the gauchos of Argentina. Yet here Kurt was penetrating the very heart of the beast. I don't know if it was this fact or something else, but I felt we shared something. I felt he respected us, perhaps understood why we had travelled almost 5000 miles to see this and to be abandoned on the ice to test our nerve, our resolve, to gamble our annual leave on something as beautiful and as pointless as climbing a mountain. Men trying to write their names on the icing of a cake on a hot summer's day.

Mick and Kurt could communicate with each other via their headsets. In the back, it was just me and Dylan uninterrupted, until Joni Mitchell arrived. Her voice was calm and beautiful, but still I felt anxious as we neared the end of the lake, the last flowing thing, a final reminder of life. The 76-mile Hubbard Glacier pushed down, its six-mile snout of ice edging slowly into the water. Chunks of ice floated in the lake, drifting, lost. I stared at the glacier, trying to get a sense of scale.

Now we could see beyond the initial skyline, to the north. In my heart, I had prayed for a hint of civilisation, another Yakutat or an old gold mining town, perhaps an abandoned shack or two. I had seen no easy way back through the country we had just flown over and I thought that the north might offer an escape route in case of an emergency, or if Kurt couldn't reach us for some reason. The view in that direction looked even lonelier. This was not a range that you passed over to find green and life-filled valleys, like in the Andes or the Alps. Instead it stretched on and on. I had wanted a test, I thought, and here it was.

The plane dipped and rose, the engine still beautiful, the timbre of its voice reassuring. Below, cotton-white glaciers curved around pyramidal peaks with walls of ice and serrated rock ridges. On the left, I recognised Mount Alverstone and Cathedral Glacier; our descent from Kennedy must come down there somewhere. It was difficult to calculate how long it would take us to return to base camp from here. It would depend on the condition of the snow, but it didn't look straightforward. Maybe four days?

Thin clouds floated below us now, casting shadows on the glacier. Kurt didn't appear to have a map. This was raw, wild flying, where you read the air, memorised landmarks, deciphered signs in the clouds, interpreted the glaciers for possible landing sites. Flying beyond the manual or the handbook. Like Eielson, Crosson, Jefford and Reeve, surviving through experience, always learning. Up here, you were always a pupil.

The curved windscreen of the plane had a perpendicular metal strip in the centre and on either side a thinner strip that ran from bottom-centre up to the top corners. Through these four triangles all I saw was a wall of snow and ice. Perhaps we are going to climb over these peaks, I mused. As time passed, Kurt made no attempt to climb; he had started strumming his knee again. I lifted my head and realised we were going to fly through a notch in the mountainside.

A few seconds later, the sound of the engine began reverberating off the walls, a deep, throaty bass. On the left, the dark cliffs looked too close. The plane twitched, ploughing through a slightly different air mass. I stared at the cracks in the rock and tried to guess what size protection you would need if you were going to climb them. The other side looked similar. I laughed to myself, a nervous laugh, a gesture belying fear. We flew out of the notch into the sun, banking leftwards into a valley lined with peaks, the glacier below a perfect white plain. Soon, I thought, we will be landing somewhere like that.

Mick turned and pointed.

'Our mountain,' he mouthed.

It was the vast north face of Mount Kennedy, our challenge for the next month.

'Looks OK,' I said flippantly, without studying it too hard.

Suddenly Kurt banked the plane to the right. I gripped the edge of the seat to steady myself, stiffening my neck, bracing myself. Through widening eyes I noticed that Mount Kennedy had now turned on its side. I felt like I was sitting in a tumbling war plane, one of those Spitfires that seemed to spiral out of control in every World War II movie ever made, black smoke trailing, a high-pitched whine, the plane accelerating towards the ground, the pilot losing consciousness, me, the navigator, trapped in the back. But then it all went calm and we were flying level again and I gathered it was all planned; Kurt needed to lose height and so had to turn tightly at the head of the dead-end valley. We sank towards the glacier.

The propeller threw snow into the air and the skis glided so smoothly that it took me several seconds to register that we had actually landed.

Kurt shut down the engine and we climbed out. It was impeccably still.

'We appear to have arrived, Andrew,' said Mick comically.

'Do you think he could have got us any closer?' I joked.

We unloaded our equipment, stacking it together in a pile. It looked no more than a couple of hours to the base of our route.

'I'm sure we were in Birmingham yesterday.'

'Let's hope we get a few weeks of weather like this,' I said.

'You could be lucky, guys,' said Kurt, smiling.

Kurt looked relaxed on the glacier. These were his mountains, and he had landed in this place before, flying in hopefuls intent on climbing the preposterous north face.

Mick took out a map and the three of us peered down.

'I could land down here if you guys can't make it back to this place,' Kurt said, pointing to the lower Cathedral Glacier. 'I have landed higher, but I don't want to if I can avoid it. You can call me up on the radio anyhow, if you're done earlier.'

'Sounds perfect,' Mick said.

'Better go get the others, in case the weather changes,' said Kurt, glancing up at the sky.

He started the engine, and soon enough the skis slid along the track he had made on landing. He accelerated away down the glacier and then off back towards civilisation. We stood still and watched the plane recede slowly into the distance, a dark insect-like shape, soon lost, the drone fading. Then nothing. A few wispy clouds lapped at the summit ridge above. In a way, just being here on this remote glacier was a personal milestone. Unlike on Fitzroy in Patagonia, where civilisation was never too far away, here we were alone, utterly alone. Small people in a big world.

12

Vertical Camping

The mildewy aroma and feeling of snug warm feet reminded me of boyhood camping trips in South Yorkshire woodland. But unfortunately, I was on a glacier and outside it was snowing hard. I remembered now how obsessive I'd been over camping, on one occasion spending the night alone in Coka Woods, the haunted woods up by the pit, where if the ghosts didn't frighten you, the tales of the knifing gypsies did, or the hooves of the galloping white horses. I'd lied to my mother, telling her I was meeting friends, so desperate was I for closeness to nature.

I punched the roof of the tent, sending snow sliding gently towards the ground, a slow murmur of crystals scraping on nylon. I felt dehydrated; a tea would sort me out. Wriggling towards the entrance without leaving my sleeping bag, I grabbed a pan, unzipped the tent. Snowflakes the size of sweet wrappers filled the sky and the mountains had vanished. I packed the pan with snow and then lit the stove.

'Morning, Andrew,' said Mick without opening his eyes.

'Morning. Good sleep?'

'Absolutely brilliant. With two kids I don't get much quality sleep at home. This is luxury.'

'It's a bit of a long way to come for a decent night's kip,' I joked. 'Tea?'

'Perfect,' Mick sighed, enjoying the extravagance.

'There's no rush today, it's snowing like mad out there.'

'Hey, you lot.' It was Chris. 'How is the Cave-Fowler tent?'

'Very good.'

'Well Spunky Duncan's tent seems to be leaking.'

'I haven't used it for ages, I remember it being fine,' said Duncan. 'I'll build a shelter once it stops snowing, just in case.'

'That's not good,' I said. 'We've got the bivvy tent if you need it.'

'We'll be fine, it's just Pasteur getting soft,' said Duncan. 'His family are founding members of the Alpine Club. He should be tough.'

'You're going in the igloo, Duncan mate, I'll go in the bivvy tent,' said Chris.

'Hey, Cavey, I can't imagine you had ancestors in the Alpine Club?' shouted Duncan.

'I don't think there were many coal-mining members back in those days; more of a gentleman's pursuit, old chap.'

Oddly enough, miners had frequently featured alongside the gentry during the early ascents in the St Elias Mountains and the Wrangell further north. Annoyed by the reluctance of the Yakutat natives, Harold Topham had hired a couple of miners to bolster his team. The first successful ascent of Mount St Elias, led by the Duke of Abruzzi, employed a miner. Further north, Dora Keene set out with a party of 10 to climb the impressive Mount Blackburn (4996 metres). After appalling weather, all but Keene and H.W. Handy, a German mining engineer, descended. The pair spent 13 days stormbound in an ice cave before successfully reaching the summit. Later, they married. Another miner, Andy Taylor, was one of the key members of the party to make the epic first ascent of Mount Logan. Taylor was also chosen by Bradford Washburn to work on the exploratory surveys of the St Elias Mountains in the 1930s, the expeditions that discovered and photographed peaks such as Mount Kennedy. We had a copy of Washburn's photograph of Kennedy with us, a laminated version that lived in the side pocket of our tent.

Snow fell quietly all day, until our tents were entirely covered, the only sign of movement being a line of footsteps to the trench we had dug for a loo. We thought the path was free of crevasses, though you could never be certain. We spent most of the day reading, in between bouts of eating. The next day we organised our equipment in weak sunshine, dividing the food into base camp stuff and mountain supplies, and checking over the ropes and hardware. Duncan cut blocks of snow and started building a wonky igloo.

It felt good to be moving at last, pushing the skis through silken snow, enchanted by the splendour of the place. Mick and I headed for a pass at the end of the glacier to get a better view of Mount Kennedy's north face, but already the aura of Kennedy kept drawing our eyes as we adjusted to the sheer scale and complexity of rock, ice and snow. It reminded me of the Eiger north face in Switzerland, an imposing pyramid of rock that looked as though it had been scraped out by an ice cream scoop, leaving a steep concave wall drooling with snow and ice. We crept along beneath ranks of modest but elegant peaks, which, like so many summits here, remained unnamed and unclimbed. We stopped at the pass and marvelled at the sea of mountains and glaciers stretching to the north and east; a wild, cease-less, cold land. Mount Logan is somewhere in that direction, I thought.

We took off our skis and sat with our backs to a gentle but icy wind. Sprawling high cirrus moved up above. I scoured what I thought to be the Tackle/Roberts route and felt disheartened by the amount of snow plastering the walls. The undersides of all the overhangs sported snow mushrooms, rows of useless ghoulish gargoyles. I passed the binoculars to Mick. It was the middle of the day, in the sun, but still it felt cold, and I wrig-gled my toes and squeezed my fingers back into the palms of my hands to stave off hints of numbness. That morning in the tent I had picked up a pan to make tea and the low tempera-tures had made it stick to the skin of my fingers.

'We're obviously on a fault line here. Most of Kennedy looks like granite, but the peaks on the right look like loose shale,' I said, pointing.

'Most of the granite looks buried. It must have been one hell of a winter – it still feels like winter. How are the bits that got frostbitten on Changabang?'

'My thumb definitely feels the cold these days. They say it's never the same, once you've suffered it.'

'Those ice cliffs at the top of the face are a bit worrying,' said Mick. 'They look substantial and are right above the Tackle/Roberts line. What do you think?'

Among most mountaineers there's an unwritten law that hanging ice cliffs, also known as seracs, are a no-go area, as they can collapse unpredictably, flattening everything in their path. Climbing underneath a big serac is like a deaf and blind man crawling across a railway track . . . you might survive. I once spent two and a half hours alone racing up a wall of ice beneath a giant serac in Chamonix. An exuberant youth, at the base I had calculated that two hours was acceptable, that it was worth it. But I'd spent each minute with my heart in my mouth and vowed never to play Russian roulette again. The Japanese and a few East European climbers have earned reputations as specialists in climbing under such lethal features; they are welcome to them. There is always an arbitrary line where a climber draws his position in relation to acceptable risk. Perhaps with age my attitude towards risk had moved, and I took comfort from this. I lived by the mantra that you listened to your inner voice for your survival.

'They don't look pretty on the right,' I said.

I traced the binoculars from the summit looking for signs, clues to feed into the rough science of calculating the odds: the colour of the ice on the serac, the angle, the size of any cracks, the evidence of debris on the ground below.

'But then again, on the left they look fairly stable, as if they haven't broken off for ages.'

'We'd be under them for a few days.'

Mount Kennedy with route marked. Triangles denote bivouac sites. Two nights were spent in bivouac 2.

'Three at least. But it's not just the seracs. It's the sheer volume of snow on the face. Compare it to Jack Tackle's photos – at least there was ice on the route then. It just looks like a load of powder snow perched on rocks now.'

'What about any other lines?'

'I can see one to the left and another to the right. The left looks harder, but the right is straight under the seracs. They're both smothered in powder. And if you look carefully, the whole face is concaved, a shallow couloir; if anything slid off those top slopes, you'd get nailed.'

Before I could go on, a giant cloud appeared, plummeting from the top of the face towards the glacier. It was an impressive avalanche, screaming down the exact route we were discussing.

I felt my stomach clench. I had overcome many hurdles since Changabang, finally finding the resolve to return to a remote, difficult climb. As the snow mushroom fell, growing and tearing at everything in its path, I felt my inner ballast shrink. Even if you survived something like that, you wouldn't want to carry on. Your clothes would be drenched. We didn't have enough time for dithering.

Mick cleared his throat. 'That is extremely worrying.'

'You know the north buttress looks brilliant further left, and much safer.'

The north buttress had first been climbed by David Seidman and Todd Thompson in 1968, by using fixed ropes and establishing camps. A great achievement at the time, it still awaited a lightweight, alpine-style ascent. Some of the world's strongest teams had failed on this, mainly due to prolonged storms, as Mark Twight had pointed out.

'I think we are thinking the same thing, Andrew.'

I felt a subtle release that Mick was not fixated on the wall to the right. 'We don't have lots of time and I really want to get to the top of something, especially after Patagonia.'

'It's always good to succeed. It makes Mr Fowler a very happy man.'

Close up, Mick was a gentle man and a superb team player.

Over the last few years, the gaze of alpinists from around the world had fallen on this slightly built, eccentric man. Mick's record in the world's mountains was exceptional. However, his understated accounts of his climbs often gave the impression that he had just taken a stroll down the high street, and in photographs he is always smiling, no matter how precarious, absurd or dangerous his position on the rock, ice or rubble. Some climbers specialised in limestone, others preferred gritstone. Mick was not fussy. For him it didn't actually matter what it was made of, but it always tasted better if no one had been there before, if his team were the first to climb it. He was the present-day Bill Tilman or Eric Shipton.

'You will now have the pleasure of seeing the Fowler on skis,' cried Mick, firing off down the slope, not nearly as badly as he made out.

On the glacier, we glided along with a gentle hiss, the light up on Kennedy exquisite, tiny cerulean shadows from the afternoon sun. I felt content now that we had a plan. I could manage hard climbing and the cold, but I didn't want to be anywhere near an avalanche. We arrived back at base camp by late afternoon. Further down the glacier, we could see the figures of Chris and Duncan heading back.

'What've you lot been up to?' asked Mick as they arrived, their chests heaving.

'The B Team has climbed a new mountain,' Duncan announced.

'Which one?'

'The mini Spunkhorn,' smirked Chris. 'We'll have to go back again to reach the main summit.'

'Excellent views from the Spunkhorn,' Duncan said. 'What do you think of the name, Andy?'

In the early 1980s a couple of friends had climbed a virgin summit in the Himalayas and called it Peak Frank Zappa. Why not? A little irreverence from time to time was healthy. If JFK could have a peak named in his honour, why not Zappa or indeed our friend 'Spunky Duncan', as Mick and Chris called him. It was better than Point 5692 Metres, surely?

That evening Chris decided to make a fish curry, and set about cutting the enormous chunk of frozen halibut with his ice axe. He looked like some starving Arctic savage killing prey, yet the dish was wonderfully tasty and the perfect meal before setting off on the north face the following day.

Next morning, I studied the photograph before leaving. This black-and-white image of Washburn's had inspired so many different people to come to this mountain over the years. I stared at the protuberances of snow, tiny pyramids that we prayed we could cut into to position our tent. Tonight's spot looked promising; after that, possible sites existed but were more spaced. I folded the photograph and placed it in the inside pocket of my jacket. For the next few days it would be our only map of this steep, cold world. I skied off after Mick, from the sun into the shade, stopping where snow had slid from above, forming a bridge across the gaping hole of the bergschrund.

'Impressive amount of snow,' said Mick as he stepped out of his skis and disappeared up to his thighs.

I dropped my pack on to the slope and then stepped from my skis too, sinking immediately almost to my waist.

'Why do we do this, Mick?' I said.

'Because it's good for us, Andy. It will make us happy afterwards.'

'It looks firmer above.'

We placed our skis together and then put on our helmets and crampons. Chris and Duncan had kindly agreed to come and collect our skis the following day, in case it snowed and they got buried. Mick tied into the ends of the two ropes without removing his gloves and then swung his rucksack on to his shoulders. He swam through the deep snow for a few minutes, trying to find something solid underfoot. He used his knees and shins against the slope, the larger surface area not sinking so far, but it was still hard work. Where the slope steepened, the depth of unconsolidated snow lessened, and as he crossed the snow bridge, I could see the picks of his ice axes biting more securely.

Mick moved quicker now, a dark shrinking figure in the white. Above him sat the first rocks, steep, slender towers, like rows of solemn men. He shouted down and I felt the rope tighten at my waist, the signal to start. The bergschrund was a line, a chance to change my mind. Yet in that moment of setting off, any doubt about what we were hoping to achieve subsided and I felt only the deep calm that accompanies commitment. We had prepared to the best of our ability and were now ready to embrace the uncertainty of the adventure, that crucial, indecipherable kernel of mountaineering. I appreciated the snug rope from above as I kicked my feet into the snow bridge, trying to avoid gazing into the void either side of me.

It was a relief to start, but within minutes all I could think of was how loose my feet felt inside my boots. Afraid of my feet becoming damaged by cold again following the Changabang climb, I had chosen a bigger pair of boots. I cursed under my breath. You tried to plan everything right and something as major as this happened. I joined Mick, took the ice screws and clipped them on to my harness, not mentioning the boots. Maybe I was overreacting; sometimes things settled down. Plus, we had to make it up to the ridge if we were to have any chance of a decent night's sleep.

I skirted around the base of the rock buttress, punching my hands and feet into the slope, pausing after about 100 feet. I squeezed my hands into fists, trying to get blood into numb fingers. Feather snow crystals floated in the air. Earlier, clouds had swirled around the upper face, but now these had gone, and when I reached the end of the rope I emerged into dazzling afternoon sun. The face was steepening now and we found more of a rhythm. After a few hours of climbing, we could see the ridge where we wanted to spend the night, perhaps 300 feet higher, out to our left on the far side of a large, steep ribbed slope.

'It looks like small powder avalanches rattle down here,' I said.

'Yes, I suppose that's what these little gullies are,' Mick said. 'Not a problem for Mr Cave.'

Mick's unrelenting enthusiasm for this world always rubbed off on me. I felt my confidence returning, though I vowed to try and do something about my damn feet once we stopped for the night.

I moved horizontally over the first rib of soft snow and then down into a scoured icy gully where snow had slid from above. I climbed up on to the top of the next snow rib and glanced back towards Mick, who hung from the belay. It was like climbing across a giant pair of frozen corduroy trousers. I placed an ice screw in the dark ice of the next channel and then on the next rib of soft snow decided to take a photo of Mick. If he was nervous, he certainly didn't show it. Through my viewfinder his poise was of someone on a family beach holiday. If he hadn't been holding the ropes, he might have given a friendly wave.

I could see the ridge itself now and hoped I had enough rope to reach it. It was worth a try, safer than standing in one of these snow chutes. I moved gingerly across deepening snow, balancing my way towards the ridge. It wasn't difficult, but it was not a place to fall. Between my legs I could see the glacier more than 1000 feet below. I planted my ice axes as high as I could, and then moved my feet up, kicking each one two or three times. Eventually I stood up on the ridge. It was just three feet wide. Though airy, it would be safe from falling debris. Below me it flattened out, became wider and looked a promising site for the tent. I moved up, stamped out a platform and then dug into the snow until I reached ice. I placed two ice screws, anchoring myself.

'This looks like a very fine campsite to me,' Mick smiled when he arrived.

'It's a camping holiday really,' I said. 'A vertical camping holiday.'

I tied off the ropes, and then joined Mick below. He had already begun using his feet to remove snow. Two hours later we had the tent up and Mick had lit the stove.

'By normal standards this is brilliant,' he announced, lying back, his head on his sleeping bag.

'Luxury camping,' I said.

We had got off to the best possible start. We drank tea, ate pasta and Parmesan and then at 7 p.m. made the prearranged call to Chris and Duncan via the radio. They were back at base camp, having reached the summit of a peak at the head of the glacier.

'Not difficult, but probably a first ascent,' Chris relayed.

'And the name?' Mick asked.

'The Spunkhorn, of course,' Chris announced gleefully.

As I searched for my knife, I wondered what the national park authorities would make of that. I cut two insoles for my boots out of the bottom of my Karrimat, leaving a couple of amusing footprint-shaped holes.

I woke the following morning with the rope digging into my ribs. Remaining tied on inside the tent meant that if anything struck from above we would at least have a chance of surviving, but it was always uncomfortable. We snoozed as the stove murmured, knowing it would take at least 40 minutes to melt enough snow to provide hot water for tea. I tuned into the sound of the burning flame, enjoying the warmth of my sleeping bag. Hopefully, today's climbing would not be desperate, though it looked a long way to the next camping spot.

We ate porridge, drank tea and then filled our water bottles. Outside, our track to the foot of the mountain was faint but visible, meandering out to the dark dot of base camp. A single herringbone cloud travelled slowly over the summit, often the harbinger of a storm. With numb fingers I packed my rucksack, put on crampons and then untangled the ropes. Mick climbed rightwards across the slope, plunging his ice axes into deep snow, until he was beneath a broken granite cliff.

'Who turned the lights off?' I said when I joined him. The

sky was suddenly darkened by swirling clouds descending towards us.

'Ah well, onwards and upwards, Andy,' said Mick cheerily.

The granite directly above was smothered in snow, numb and lifeless. Instead, I climbed up a little and then traversed on to a mosaic of green ice peppered with small rocks. I swung my pick, but it bounced like a bullet from a castle wall. I struck again and the ice splintered, large glass lumps skidding and then rolling down towards the glacier. Third time lucky, I thought, as the pick punctured the ice with a reassuring thud. I moved up, settled my feet and placed an ice screw, the earlier tension evaporating, my shoulders loosening. Higher up, the angle eased and I moved more quickly up to a belay on an island of rock. A single snowflake fell. Within a few minutes it began snowing heavily. Mick arrived, his hood up, snow stuck to the arms of his jacket.

'Just like Scotland,' I said.

'Yes, but I seem to be breathing more heavily for some reason,' he said. 'It must be doing us some good.'

'Good training for something,' I said.

The further we climbed up the face, the stronger the wind became and the thicker the snow. By mid-afternoon a maelstrom enveloped us and we began to worry about where we might spend the night. We huddled together hanging from two ice screws, staring at the photo of the face. I didn't mind carrying on as long as we could be certain of a safe place to stay. Small snow slides had started to sweep down either side of us, but now they were increasing in size. In the poor visibility they were impossible to anticipate and made me nervous.

'We've climbed about nine hundred metres, according to my altimeter,' I said.

Mick pointed to the right.

'That spur there,' he said. 'It doesn't look that far away, it may be a possibility.'

The inserts in my boots worked perfectly, yet the sheer volume of snow on the face made the climbing insecure.

Occasionally a toehold collapsed and my weight suddenly lurched on to the ice axes. About 100 feet away from Mick I stopped, wanting to place an ice screw. It took so long to dig through the snow to the ice that I almost gave up. But we couldn't afford an accident up here. The snow slides crashed harder now and lasted longer, racing past like sand, the spray covering my face and freezing my eyes. I lowered my head, gripped my ice axes and prayed for a lull. At last I managed to get a screw to bite into some ice. I could no longer see Mick and we couldn't hear each other as the storm intensified. I set off again. We had to find somewhere to stop.

'Is this the right way?' I yelled into the swirling whiteness. I couldn't see or hear anything.

I climbed on through the spiralling snow until I was beside a small protuberance. That is a possibility, I thought, just as a huge snow slide careered by. Jesus. I moved up on to the small spur and peered down the other side. The face suddenly steepened. This was it, a dead end.

'It will have to do,' I growled.

It was hard to believe the day had dawned so gently.

I took off my rucksack and clipped it in carefully; if I dropped that, we'd be done for. Without the tent and the stove, you wouldn't last long here.

Ice around the sheath meant the rope caught in the belay device as I pulled it in. An almighty crash sounded out to the right. I shortened my neck, held my breath and closed my eyes, fearing the worst. I felt nothing. It was difficult to know if it was thunder or an avalanche. I opened my eyes and carried on pulling in the rope.

Mick appeared like an apparition, the red of his jacket encrusted in rime ice.

'Better get on with it, I guess,' he shouted through the eddying storm.

Taking turns, we beat the tiny snow spur with our ice axes. After about an hour, we cut into the tougher snow-ice. Avalanches cascaded either side of us now with a new ferocity.

We had the ropes tied to ice screws up above, but I wanted to place a screw by our feet to anchor the tent. The snow-ice was too soft and it ripped out repeatedly. Carefully we put up the tent, tensioned it to the two ropes above and then crawled inside, exhausted.

Hauling loads during the first ascent of Mount St Elias, led by the Duke of Abruzzi, 1897

Tlingit Indians kayaking across Yakutat Bay, 1902

Legendary glacier pilot Bob Reeve with his wife Jan, 1937

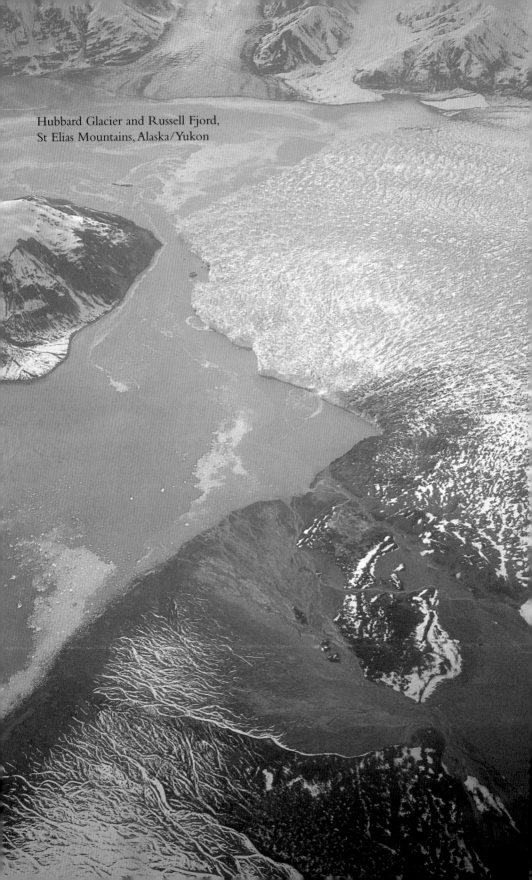

Hubbard Glacier and Russell Fjord,
St Elias Mountains, Alaska/Yukon

Mick Fowler meets a polar bear, Juneau airport, Alaska

Kurt Gloyer, ace mountain pilot, St Elias Mountains

Andy, Kurt and his Cessna

Eiger of the Yukon: North buttress of Mount Kennedy

Andy climbing Mount Kennedy's
north buttress. Day One of the
first alpine-style ascent.

Mick heats his inner boot on the stove
during the thirty-six hour storm

Day Four: The end of the storm. Andy
stands where the tent had rested.

Andy with headwall above.
Evening of Day Four.

Day Five: Andy mixed-climbing in the black diorite band

(*Main picture*) Day Six: Mick leaves the fifth bivouac on Mount Kennedy's north buttress

Mick shields the sun approaching
the summit of Mount Kennedy

Andy and Mick on the summit of Mount Kennedy

The team at basecamp: (*left to right*) Duncan Tunstall, Chris Pasteur, Kurt Gloyer and Mick Fowler

Bill Pilling

Andy Selters

Andy making the final tenuous moves
of the serious gritstone route, End of
the Affair, Curbar, Derbyshire. E8 6c.

13

The Edge

I woke up when it was dark. I could not hear the sound of the rushing snow, and the silence comforted me until I looked at my watch. Six o'clock: it should be light by now. I shone my head torch against the tent walls and saw how narrow they had become. Panic rose in my chest. We've been totally buried. I sat up and went to open the tent door, but stopped. If we had been buried, snow would pour in endlessly.

I knelt there, ice from the skin of the tent falling on to my neck and melting. A small heap of perfect snow crystals covered the floor of the tent, stuff that had forced its way through the small gaps in the zipper where the ropes to our waists exited. I pushed at the tent fabric, hoping to move some of the snow, but when I released my hand the side walls sprang back in. I pressed at the tent door repeatedly and then moved the zipper up to the top. I opened it a fraction, but snow fell in immediately, so I closed it. The flakes sparkled like diamonds in the beam of my light. I pushed at the fabric with force now, managing to move the wall of snow away from the tent. I peered through a small hole in the zip and could just see out to the slope above. We would be OK.

I lit the stove and slumped back, listening to the drone. After breakfast we could put on our boots and mittens and try and dig out the entrance, find out what sort of day it was.

'This is obviously a spat of the infamous St Elias weather,' I said, a little glum.

'We do like a challenge, Andrew. It's good for us,' Mick said, sounding like some bonkers Victorian missionary.

'Mick, it's freezing and we're sat on an island of snow, three thousand and whatever feet above the glacier. I don't know what's good about that.'

'It's character-building.'

'I did all my character building in Patagonia in the wind. I don't need any more here.'

'Think of the retrospective pleasure,' said Mick, sipping his tea.

'I want to climb this thing, get it over with, and talking of pleasure . . .'

'Talking of pleasure, let's get some porridge ready. I'm ravenous.'

Suddenly the radio crackled into life.

'Morning, A Team, this is Biffers at base camp. Do you read me, over?'

'Good morning, Chris, this is Mick. What's the weather like down there, over?'

'It's snowing like hell, has been all night. Where are you two?'

'We reckon we've climbed about nine hundred metres, so more or less halfway up. We're perched on a small snow crest to the right of the main ridge.'

'Sounds fun.'

'Well we haven't been hit by anything too big yet, though they seem to come quite close.'

'What's the climbing been like?'

'Not difficult, but serious. What about you lot, what have you been up to?'

'We're keen to try the east ridge of Mount Kennedy, if it ever stops snowing.'

'Sounds good. We'll have a chat up here and decide what to do. We'll call you again at seven this evening.'

'Right-oh, chaps, speak later.'

The last syllable faded like the final note of a song. Briefly, we had enjoyed the company of our team mates, but then they had vanished in an instant. Silence filled the tent.

After breakfast, I went out and began clearing away snow from the small gap between us and the ice slope. It was light enough and shifted easily with the side of my boot, but infuriatingly, snow kept sliding down from above, refilling the gap. After 20 minutes, out of breath, I stopped for a while, small avalanches screaming past either side of the tent. We were stranded, marooned in an ocean of white waves. It continued to snow, broad, fat flakes. The visibility was nonexistent in every direction. The sudden sound of a much larger avalanche crashing down the face to the right unnerved me further still. If anything substantial hit us, I knew we'd struggle to stay balanced here.

'That sounded quite big,' said Mick, peering out from the tent.

'Good decision climbing this line, rather than on the right,' I said. 'You couldn't survive over there with things that size coming down.'

'I agree. Cashew nut?'

Mick held out three nuts in his hand.

'Is that it?' I said.

'Well, we might be here a while by the looks of it.'

I took off my glove and reached down. I put a nut into my mouth and gently ground it into a paste.

'Do you ever wish you had gone on a beach holiday, Mick?' I asked, just as yet another big snow slide rushed past.

'I find them dull. Beaches with cliffs are OK, I suppose.'

'I was thinking more ice creams, chicks, cool lager in the bar, that sort of thing. Not great big tottering piles of rubble by the sea.'

'You can't beat a good British sea cliff adventure.'

'I'd probably swap it for here right now, that's for sure. I'd swap right here for anything.'

Using the lid from our pan, I scooped as much snow off the tent as possible and then went inside. We spent the morning reading. Mick had a racy thriller. I read a small book about community and identity by an anthropologist called Anthony Cohen. Reading was the best way we had invented to stop thinking about things. You could ignore the void in an instant. 'You can live a lifetime and, by the end of it, know more about other people than you know about yourself,' wrote Beryl Markham, the pioneering pilot. 'You learn to watch people, but you never watch yourself because you strive against loneliness. If you read a book, or shuffle a deck of cards, or care for a dog, you are avoiding yourself. The abhorrence of loneliness is as natural as wanting to live at all. If it were otherwise, men would never have bothered to make an alphabet, nor to have fashioned words out of what were only animal sounds, nor to have crossed continents – each man to see what the other looked like.'

I tried to work out the essence of what Cohen was saying about groups and behaviour based on fieldwork on Shetland. I was settled into my book when the violent sound of hurtling snow bolted me up to sitting, back arched like a frightened cat.

'Shit,' I said, dropping the book.

The tent started to vibrate, and both walls squeezed towards my head. Suddenly the world went black. We had become one with the mountain, swallowed up by tumbling snow. The tent poles began to rattle. I clasped my hands together and shut my eyes tightly.

A few seconds later the shaking stopped and the light returned. We were still there: two frightened birds in a nylon cage.

Mick exhaled slowly. We stared at each other, Mick with a look of resignation. I felt the last surges of adrenalin like sharp barbs being thrust into my chest and arms. There was nowhere to hide.

'The beach,' I said. 'I'm going to the fucking beach next time.'

Even if we survived all these snow slides, we hadn't got much food left, four days in total after today. The memories of the suffering and hunger endured on Changabang came back, raw and clear. I felt cracks in my resolve. All the small steps back on the road to this place began to crumble, the fragile solidity turning to ash. Patagonia, Norway and the great start here, all slipping away. Mick saw the nervousness in my eyes. I needed a diversion, a story, something to escape this place.

'You got any good projects on the sea cliffs?' I said to fill the silence.

'There is a great challenge left on the mighty Bempton. You would love it.'

'Bempton, that place near Filey on the east coast?'

'That's the one. Superb. Four hundred feet straight out of the sea.'

'I thought it was collapsing *into* the sea.'

'It's not that bad.'

'Have you climbed there already?'

'Yes, but the main challenge remains.'

'Which is?'

'To climb on the highest part of the cliff.'

'I know somebody who went there and refused to climb at all, reckoned it looked like death.'

'Honestly, it's not that bad,' Mick smiled. 'With a boat, on a calm day we'd manage it. And it would be a beach holiday.'

He had such a great smile and such energy, he won everyone over. That's how he persuades people to pay their tax bills, I mused: 'Pay up, sir, or I'm going to take you rock-climbing at Bempton and frighten you to death!'

'Another nut?'

'Why not, I've heard the oil in them is good for your complexion.'

'There you go, a bit of sustenance.'

'Five? Wow. Must be my birthday. Did I ever tell you about the first time I met Victor?'

'No, go on.'

'He told me I could stay at his house if I was ever passing through London. On my way to the Alps that winter, I turned up.

I had never climbed in the Alps in winter before and was eager to pick up any tips. We came back from the pub late and he started asking me what gloves I was using. He said he'd discovered some amazing thin ones and suggested we compare. He opened the lid of an enormous chest freezer and started passing me frozen chickens, tubs of ice cream, frozen peas. After a bit, he told me to swap and try his. Then I confessed that I was taking a pair of my mam's tights to wear under my fleece trousers for extra insulation. He disappeared into his gear store and came back with a pair of fishnet stockings. He reckoned I should try them underneath the tights. And he was right: my legs were red hot. But as I was putting the chickens back into the bottom of the freezer, I heard someone walking around in the next room and suddenly panicked. I mean, think about it: I'd got on thin white gloves, fishnet stockings and was bent over a freezer next to a man I had only met once before, a man who'd been at school with Prince Charles.'

'Did you wear the tights on the mountain?' Mick asked.

'Yes, I soloed a route on the north face of the Courtes in them, with fleece and Gore-Tex over the top, obviously.'

'What were they like?'

'Amazing. Too warm, to be honest.'

We spent the afternoon telling stories; it kept the fear at bay. It was as if speaking of others' misfortunes made our situation more bearable. In the afternoon Mick went out and cleared away some snow. There was virtually no wind, but the snow kept falling. When he came in, we ate supper and then called the others on the radio.

'We've had over three feet down here at base camp and it's still coming,' Duncan said.

Snow is the reason why people have failed here, I thought. Not just the ridiculous amounts of unconsolidated snow that you have to try and climb up, but the heaps of spindrift and terrorising avalanches. Why else had such talented alpinists failed here over the years? Doug Chabot and Alex Lowe, Jack Tackle and Jack Roberts, these people were not your average climbers. Between them, they had climbed Everest and countless other lesser known but more difficult peaks, and yet they had been forced to retreat from this face. So might we. In fact, after the radio call, Mick broached the subject of descending. It was not like him.

We simply didn't have the food to stay for much longer; we'd cut it fine with seven days' worth anyhow. I knew that he would want to climb back up once the weather stabilised, though. I could see the logic in this, but dreaded the thought of reclimbing the 900 metres to here. Plus, I worried we would struggle to find abseil anchors, any solid ice being submerged under a deep layer of unreliable, cruddy snow. It might not have been technical climbing up to this point, but we were now incredibly committed.

'Let's see what tomorrow brings,' I said nervously, as we lay back to try and get some sleep.

It had seemed such fun, the first time I had bivouacked in snow. I was 17 years old, and a bunch of us from the Barnsley Mountaineering Club had spent the night freezing below Kinder Downfall in Derbyshire. Now, I wondered how long you could keep doing this before the novelty wore off. Not much longer, I concluded.

It had stopped snowing the next morning, but you couldn't see anything; thick mist churned slowly around our small blue tent.

'I don't like the way these slopes are loaded,' Mick said. 'What do you think?'

'I don't know. It's difficult to see what's above us. I suppose we can set off and see what it feels like. We can always retreat to here.'

'It's so hard to predict what is lurking up there.'

'If we descend we will be exposed to avalanches. Perhaps if we make it up to the rock band, things will improve.'

'I hate dithering,' Mick scowled.

'Let's rub our noses in it. If we don't like it, we can get the hell out of here.'

Mick warmed his inner boots over the flame of the stove

and then got ready. The air was pregnant with dread. I untangled the frozen ropes whilst Mick put on his crampons. We both moved slowly, as if purposely delaying our moment of departure. It had been a precarious place to sleep, but we had survived here through the worst of the storm, and leaving its sanctuary was more difficult than we'd anticipated. I kept my ears alert for the noise of crashing snow as Mick booted the ice with his crampons, and let the rope inch through my hands as he crept up into the ghostly gloom.

Once Mick yelled he was safe, I followed on, trying to place my feet where his had been, my lungs burning. With barely a word, I carried on past Mick into deeper, more unstable snow. If I kept moving, I didn't have to think about things, I theorised, but my shoulders remained hunched, my stomach tense. I climbed cautiously and then paused below a much steeper section. Amidst the fear, I found myself marvelling at the snow formations above, sculpted by the cold hand of the wind. Pure and fragile art. I stood there, suddenly realising I'd have to climb straight up through it.

There was grace and style needed to climb even this stuff. White silken powder, impossibly balanced. I kicked a foot, rested my knee against the slope and stood up, softly pushing my ice axe higher up into the snow, crystals billowing, dusting my cheeks.

The steep curve of the slope above worried me. An attractive cornice, its beauty in no doubt, hung above. But was it a trap? I had no protection, nothing to break my fall, just Mick holding the rope 40 metres below. In my heart it felt right, but I knew how much surface tension could hide in a slope just below the lip of a cornice, where the wind had packed snow crystals into a tightly bonded layer of slab. I leaned forward softly and lunged my axe towards the cornice, trying to weaken it. I struck again and this time a heap of snow released, tumbling down towards the glacier. I stayed still and then climbed up a little, settled my feet again and chopped some more. I wanted to reduce its size and menace. I thrust again and again, like plunging daggers into a fallen bull. When satisfied, I moved up gently, keeping my body weight even through all four limbs, as if climbing on to a mined bank of sand.

By the time Mick reached the stance, sun the colour of weak tea was streaking across the slope. The cloud still boiled above us, but it definitely felt brighter and it lightened our mood. Mick even posed for a photograph before continuing up more unconsolidated snow above. Though not technical, the climbing looked serious. Essentially, he climbed a 200-foot pitch without protection. Placing ice screws at the belays took him 20 minutes, instead of the usual two. He had to dig a deep hole in the snow and then, at full stretch, only just touched the ice. It was tedious and we both longed to be on steeper, more interesting terrain.

After hours of punching our way strenuously up the face, we stood in a hollow on the edge of a huge fan-shaped sweep of ice. I pulled out the photo we had of the mountain, the image that had first inspired us to come to this place, and passed it to Mick.

'On the far side of this snow field there should be a little snow spur. Hopefully there will be a place to stop.'

'Sounds promising,' I said. 'But where the hell is that lot coming from?'

'What?'

'This face we've got to cross, there's snow spewing all over it. I just hope no rocks are mixed in with it.' I stared down at the glacier. You could just make out the crevasses behind base camp, 4000 feet below. 'How good is that belay?'

'Two ice screws,' Mick said.

'I'll be glad when this dangerous walking is over.'

'Tell me about it.'

I climbed up to the edge of where the snow was streaming by and waited for a lull. I worried that because of the collapsing snow underfoot, I wouldn't be able to move quickly enough. If an avalanche came, I couldn't get out of the way in time. Also, the ropes were now covered in snow and were heavy, tugging like a reluctant dog at my waist. I put up my hood, tightened my gloves and set off. I moved out tentatively, craning my head from time to time. After just 10 metres, the first wave arrived, the snow showering me completely. I closed my eyes and held my breath until it had passed. I shook my head, spat out the snow and set off again. Within a minute, the next wave came, and with much more power. It poured over me, pushing at my arms, forcing me to kick my feet deeper to stay balanced. I leaned in and hung on, like a crab clinging to the beach in a breaking wave. When it stopped, I pulled down my glasses; they were packed with snow and my eyelids had frozen together. I rubbed each eye clear with my glove, then started moving again. I was too committed to return now. I kept my head up, fighting the panic. I couldn't afford to fall here. Just keep going. I punched across the slope, but stopped after 30 paces, panting.

I peered up and saw the next wave, already airborne, jetting over the top of the granite buttress 500 feet above. This was a monster. I set off again, moving as fast as I could, but my lungs burned with the effort and I knew I could not escape. I stopped, and dug my feet as hard as I could into the slope, fear pumping to the very ends of my fingers. I tugged at the zip under my neck and then beat each axe into the sugary snow. I thought of turning and glancing at Mick, to check if he knew what was happening, but a loud hiss made me bow my head and grip my axes.

This slide was heavier than the others, and the snow quickly formed a wedge between me and the mountain. As the wedge expanded, I knew I had only seconds to react. I lifted one leg from the slope, hoping that would allow snow to flow down away from me. Nothing happened, and the snow fell in more violently now. Instinctively I removed my right arm so that I was balancing on just one leg and one arm. It worked. The snow began to gush around the edge of my body, though my leg trembled under the strain. I had only one thought: if there are any rocks or ice in this, I am dead.

As the slide faded, I kicked my other foot back into the slope and stood there motionless. Soon it stopped altogether. Up above I saw a tiny patch of blue sky. Would fate allow me to pass? Despite the suffering, I wanted this mountain now, this strange, unfathomable thing called 'the climb'. We had given so much of ourselves. I stared down and realised my arms had become welded to the slope, my ice axes and fore-arms hidden within the milk whiteness. I wriggled them and after some effort wrenched them free. Some protection would have been nice, but the incentive to get out of there was more of a pull, and I set off again, climbing 50 feet towards a small piece of ice on the other side. Arriving, I placed some ice screws, clipped in my rucksack and then shouted for Mick to start.

As I pulled in the ropes, I remembered how little food remained in our rucksacks and reflected that we had to go on. We had no choice now.

'That was grim,' said Mick, shaking his hood.

'Grim? It was fucking insane,' I said bitterly.

It was hard to know what Mick was thinking, his eyes hidden behind his sunglasses.

'It looks better now. I reckon we should look for some-where to stay before we get to the rock band.'

'Yes,' I said, squeezing my hands, trying to warm them. 'Do your best.'

We had survived the crossing of the slope, and there was little point wasting time reliving it.

Whilst Mick climbed, I thought of the early pioneers and what they had achieved with their clothing and equipment: Harold Topham attempting Mount St Elias using Whymper tents, weighing 33lb each. I had seen these canvas and wooden shelters in a museum and been shocked; they reminded me of the tents we had made as kids from clothes horses and sacks in the back garden. We had been pummelled by storms and spindrift, but hopefully after an hour or so we would be warm and start to dry out a little. A hundred years ago, even 50, you simply could not have afforded to get drenched like that and then spend the night out. Even in the relatively short time I had been climbing, the clothing and tents for this type of adventure had improved enormously, thank goodness.

I broke out in a smile when I saw Mick and the place he

had found for us to spend the night. With an hour's work it would be easily big enough for the tent, and behind him the sun had broken through the cloud.

'Do you think we can reach the summit tomorrow?' I asked.

'In theory. It does seem to be a big mountain, though.'

A scrap of blue sky appeared above us now, and I felt buoyed. We can do this bugger, I know we can, I thought. Whatever happened the following day, it would be a long one. The line we were following up the face had looked elegant from the ground, yet the climbing itself had been stressful and dangerous, and we lamented the fact that we had done virtually no technical climbing. Hopefully tomorrow, up in the rock band, that would change.

14

Atonement

Unable to reach any more porridge with the spoon, I wiped the inside of the mug clean with my finger. I sat there, sucking my finger, eager to soak up every last drop. Outside it was perfectly still, but the sublime light of the previous evening had gone; instead a veil of thin grey cloud hovered just above the rock band. We took turns to kneel on the tent, trying to reduce the bulk before stuffing it into a rucksack. Each morning it increased in size as ice built up in the fabric, the moisture from our breath and steam from the stove frozen. Excited by the prospect of some steeper, technical climbing, we set off diagonally across firmer snow-ice, aiming for the base of a weakness in the rock band. I was not in this game for the suffering. I realized that what actually motivated me was climbing hard, as light and as fast as possible. Like Mick, I abhorred labouring up dangerous slopes. Over the past few days we had found ourselves committed on ground both of us detested. Usually we chose steep routes, in part because snow couldn't accumulate. But here, even slopes greater than 60 degrees collected snow in a way they never did in the Himalayas or the Alps.

Mick beat his mittens together, trying to warm his hands, and then started up the black rock band. If we could crack the next 500 feet, we'd have a chance of reaching the summit. Staring around, I realised that Tackle and Roberts must have retreated down here somewhere during their epic outing. After enduring nine freezing days on the face, they spent a further two days descending to the glacier in a storm. The thought of going down from here filled me with horror. It would require numerous awkward diagonal abseils, if we could find any anchors, that was. We'd have no choice but to recross those lethal, snow-bombarded slopes too.

By the time Mick reached the belay it had begun to snow again, and I felt a sharp chill pinch the end of my nose.

'It's like being back in Scotland,' I said, approaching Mick's stance.

'I thoroughly enjoyed myself, Andrew, though it did make me breathe rather hard.' He beamed behind his dark glasses.

'I know what you mean,' I said. 'It feels so much higher than a four-thousand-two-hundred-metre peak; it feels like we're in the Himalayas.'

We weren't the only ones to have experienced this. During the first ascent of Mount St Elias, the Duke of Abruzzi's team commented that they suffered more distress here than when climbing at higher altitudes in the Andes. Later, scientists described a general compression of the atmosphere around the poles, meaning that thinner air is found here than at the same height in the tropics.

I started slowly up the fractured wall behind Mick, clawing away the snow, searching for any slots to hook. I spotted one and smashed the blade at it, but it ripped out. The action of the steel scuffing the stone gave a brief smell of charred wood, and a fine black dust settled on the snow. I hooked the blade behind a small flake instead and then jumped up each foot in turn before standing in balance. I felt my gaze sharpen. This was why we climbed. I reached over to the left and flicked a sling over a sharp finger of rock, clipped in the rope and then packed a handful of snow behind to help stick the sling in place. I glanced between my legs. Mick stood patiently, snow swirling around his red torso. I moved into a shallow groove, testing each hook of the ice axe before committing to it. At the top of the groove, I pushed my back and shoulders against the wall, trying to rest. I let my breathing calm and then swung up to a small stance, tied off the ropes and clipped in my rucksack. Barring any more hideous storms, this whole project now seemed possible.

'Excellent challenging exercise, Andrew. Nothing better,' Mick called up as he climbed.

'Turned out nice again,' I said as he arrived, snow covering his hood.

'It is always a pleasure to see the Cave climb with such smoothness and skill.'

'I enjoyed it. So much easier than those gruelling slopes yesterday. Another rope length and it should ease off.'

Mick pulled a face, unconvinced. He took the gear and started up the steep wall above. I noticed how efficient he was; every movement measured, each stab of the crampon solid, the axes sinking as deep as he could get them. You didn't survive 30 years in places like this through luck alone. When you listened to Mick recounting his previous ascents, you could be forgiven for thinking he'd been for a stroll. He was the master of understatement, never showy, his tone reserved. As an insider, though, you understood the context of his message. In truth he was one of the best mountaineers of the twentieth century, somebody who had stretched the boundaries of what was possible. And he was showing few signs of slowing down.

It was another two hours before we emerged on to the upper face. The sun lit a spectacular patch of floating snowflakes, a small cloud of hovering golden butterflies. I had never seen anything like it. Behind, the colossal face of the mountain fell away before fading into a chaos of twisted green and blue ice cliffs. I glanced up, wondering where we would spend the night; we needed to get a move on. I took the crumpled photograph of the face from my pocket and tried to work out where we were. It didn't look hopeful. We climbed from one half-promise to another. The sky had cleared completely now, but I felt tense.

Mick climbed a steep rib plastered in snow, his crampons scratching like sharp knives over glass. He placed a hexcentric into a crack and then smashed at it with his hammer, each thud flashing across the face. He clipped in the rope and then wedged himself into a niche, trying to regain his breath, contemplating an awkward step above. Much higher, to his right, I could just make out the fabled hanging ice cliffs. The steel-blue ice glinted in the afternoon sun, and though I couldn't detect any cracks, the cliffs definitely looked worth avoiding. Suddenly the gap between Mick and the ice cliffs turned white; it was a giant powder avalanche screaming towards us. I cowered, hunching my shoulders, until I realised it was actually safely to our right, charging towards our original objective, the Tackle/Roberts line. Engrossed in the climbing, Mick didn't even notice the incident. It might have been quicker to move diagonally up the slope, but that confirmed that we had to stay on this relatively protected rock rib.

'Did you see the rhino?' I asked when I got to him.

'What?'

'The white rhino. A mini avalanche that hurtled down the face over there.'

'No. Thank God we're over here.'

I started climbing directly above Mick, thinking I might find a place we could stop about 100 feet higher, just above a small tower. After 20 feet, a clean-cut arête presented itself and I had to make a decision about which side to climb. I pulled myself up and around to the left, then followed a shallow groove. Soon, though, the rock reared up. I ran my ice axe backwards and forwards above my head, clearing the snow, searching for something to hook my pick on to. Useless. Instead, I climbed out rightwards to the edge of the tower, my feet teetering on flakes the width of a coin. I was a long way above the last piece of protection and my face started to burn with the stress. I glanced up. It looked harder than anything we had done so far.

'Watch me here,' I called.

I hooked my right axe on the edge of the tower and leaned left, hopping my right foot up high. As I stood up, the crampon points started to shake. Suddenly I lost my nerve. Something didn't seem right. This is too hard and scary, I told myself. I moved back into the groove, stepped down and leaned my head against the rock. I was tired now.

'Shit. This might be wrong,' I said.

Mick said something, but I couldn't really hear. I climbed back down awkwardly and then crept gingerly out right. It was less steep and I made it to the top of the tower, but there was nowhere to sleep. I hauled in the ropes, feeling exhausted and hungry. We took it in turns to lead out the rope, the sun sinking, the temperature falling. The light was exquisite, but I didn't care.

'I reckon with some work we'd manage over there,' Mick said, pointing to a slender ledge on the left edge of the rib.

We set to work chopping into the slope and building up the outside edge of the ledge. We tied the top of the tent into rocks above, took off our crampons and crawled inside.

'Thank God for that,' I said. 'But I really thought we would make it to the top today.'

Mick passed me the food bag for day five, which meant that, after tonight's meal, we had food for just one full day plus the bag we'd marked as 'day seven etc.'. The 'etc.' belying the fact that it contained just a couple of packets of noodles, tea, milk and some sugar. It would last us two days at a push, plus a day or so of drinking tea. We had only actually been climbing for three and a half days, but the storm cost us a day and plastered everything in snow, so we'd climbed slower than we'd hoped. As soon as we finished eating, I lay down. If weather prevented Kurt flying in to the south side of the mountain to meet us, we were in a very serious predicament. I closed my eyes and thought about Elaine, how much I missed her. I thought of my parents, my brother Jonny and sister Maria, but before long I fell into a deep sleep.

'What date is it, Mick?' I said when I woke the next morning.

'The thirtieth, I think. It's our sixth day on the mountain.'

'I'm sure Barnsley play at Wembley today.'

'What's the occasion?'

'They're in the play-off final. If they win, they'll go up to the Premiership.'

I finished my tea, and then went outside. The sky had cleared completely, a big cobalt canvas above the white-toothed horizon. The vicious cold snapped at my shoulders and legs. I put on my balaclava and duvet jacket; I had no more clothes to put on now. While Mick dismantled our tent, I took a small file and sharpened our ice axe picks and crampon points, blunted by all the rock the previous day. The small filings spilled out over the black of my gloves and then disappeared into the frozen ground, the smell of metal caught in my nostrils reminding me of something. Yes, metalwork class at school, and Mr Cooper in his brown smock: good teacher, moustache, trusting us to use the lathes and drills; forgiving when we heated up twopence pieces, smashing them as flat and as wide as we could; understanding when I stole David Cleaver's poker, filed off his name and put mine on. He'd heard I'd become a climber and got decent at it. Old Cooper, he'd be proud of me here, filing the ice axes in the middle of Alaska.

'You ready?'

'I think so.'

I climbed as fast as I could, moving the balaclava over my mouth; it was harder to breathe but warmed the air. I placed an ice screw, then climbed until the rope ended and placed another. A lone figure dramatically silhouetted down on the ridge: Mick, preparing to leave the tiny ledge where we'd spent the night. As he moved up, I realised my toes were utterly frozen and started wiggling them. The thumb frostbitten on Changabang had become wooden too, and I beat it against my right hip. Wembley: that would have been brilliant. My team on the big stage; who'd have thought it? I'd sacrificed so many special things over the years for the mountains: friends' weddings; birthdays; college essays; at least one girlfriend. Perhaps it was essential to make sacrifices in order to be decent at something. I didn't know. You made a decision, lived by it, did the best you could.

Unsure about all the loose snow on the fan-shaped slope,

we edged leftwards on to a ridge. We were in the sun at last, and the view behind us was stunning. Believing we were just a few hours from the summit, I started to hum a tune, but the mild celebrations were premature. The ridge was delicate, exposed and time-consuming.

'Do you think they got the height of this thing right?' I asked.

'The Fowler body is finding it challenging. Hopefully my wife will be thrilled with the weight loss.'

Eventually we reached the final triangular face, a freezing wind buffeting us and hurling snow against our faces. My legs pierced the snow, up to my knees. All the way up this damn mountain the temperatures had been consistently low, and this meant that the snow remained infuriatingly unconsolidated. It wasn't difficult terrain now, but we continued to place protection on the occasional small islands of granite.

'I don't trust this slope,' I said.

'I agree,' said Mick. 'Let's stay cautious.'

Mick climbed up above me, his body shielding the bright disc of the sun, an orange glow etched around his head and shoulders. A little higher the angle eased and we moved together until we were beneath the final gentle slope leading to the summit. We packed away the frozen ropes, and I set out in front. The stout Mount Logan hung on the horizon, and 6000 feet below us was the barely discernible dot of base camp. The snow was hard now, and squeaked each time our crampons made contact. Free of the rope, I lost myself in the rhythm of that final climb. Before long, I saw the deep blue of the sky surrounding the summit, that final point. My throat tightened and I felt my eyes moisten at the edges. We had done it. I climbed over the last small, steep step of ice on to the very top and waited for Mick.

'Always a pleasure, Andrew,' he said, taking my hand and squeezing hard.

'Bloody brilliant,' I said, my voice faltering.

We put down our packs. White pyramids of ice surrounded us on all sides, lifeless but invigorating. No city lights, not a farm or field in view. It was a freezing, soul-stirring vista of unlimited possibility. The world was indeed a big place if you searched for it. Utter silence, except for the wind scraping against the hood of my jacket.

A week earlier, from the glacier below, we had traced a thin white line of snow and ice, hoping that it would lead us to the summit. Now here we were. The steeper face, further right, had been our original goal, and had conditions been better it might have suited us more. You took a chance and tried your best. The margin between success and failure was slim sometimes.

In Patagonia we had found a great line, but I had lost my nerve and we had abandoned it just below the summit. Here, though, I had felt the desire return, and the nerve. And despite appalling snow conditions and a terrifying storm, we had done it. I realised how far I had travelled since Changabang. Mick had returned to the big mountains with seemingly little hesitation, but I wasn't that robust. For the first time, perhaps the skill of compartmentalising things, common among successful mountaineers, had eluded me. Brendan's death had forced me to confront the real dangers of the sport and the damage such a loss inflicts on family and friends.

Just along the ridge were Mount Alverstone and Mount Hubbard, peaks that straddled the border between Canada and America. It was funny how arbitrary it was; they were just beautiful mountains in a vast wild space; who owned them meant nothing to us. The oil beneath the ice, that was what people got excited about, the undiscovered dollars. The wildness, the remoteness, this just got in the way. First they had hunted for fur, and now it was oil. We had climbed the north buttress of Mount Kennedy, and we had climbed in good style, left no trace behind, nothing but footprints, which would melt and disappear, a few urine stains that would be buried by snow. But I knew that our jackets, our ropes, our plastic boots were all made from oil, if you got down to it. We had flown from Birmingham to the glacier below the mountain. No matter what you did, you got tangled up in it all somehow.

It was odd to think that Senator Bobby Kennedy had been up here, burying mementos as a tribute to his dead brother, John. Three years later, of course, he had been assassinated too. A couple of mountain-lovers shot dead on the street. The Inaugural Medallion probably lay somewhere in the snow beneath our feet.

I sat on my rucksack, switched on the radio.

'This is Andy and Mick on Mount Kennedy. Gulf Air, do you read me?'

After a long silence I tried again.

'This is Andy Cave and Mick Fowler on the summit of Mount Kennedy. Can you hear me?'

Mick looked at me silently.

'I don't fancy the walk,' I said.

The radio crackled and then burst into life.

'Hey, Andy, this is Kurt. Where the hell are you guys? Did you say you're on the summit? Over.'

Kurt sounded as jubilant as we were and promised that he would try his best to fly into the lower Cathedral Glacier the following evening and pick us up. If he couldn't reach us there, we would be in grave difficulty. With current soft snow conditions, we reckoned it would take four days to get back to base camp, where all our glorious food was waiting. We tied back into one of the ropes and set off, facing into the slope, carefully climbing down a steep ridge of névé and then over a bergschrund to where the angle eased. That section had been the hardest part of the mountain's first ascent, and providing we followed the best route, we didn't expect anything too difficult ahead. We waded through deep snow just below the west ridge and then moved down easier slopes towards the upper Cathedral Glacier.

For the first time in five days we removed our harnesses and didn't have to worry about dropping a boot or the food bag. While the stove melted snow, we put up the tent. Everything felt easy compared to what we had been through.

Up above us sat Mount Alverstone, which reminded me of the normal route up Mont Blanc. It looked like a good thing to ski.

'It's my birthday tomorrow,' I said. 'If Kurt picks us up as planned, in theory we could be swilling ales back in Yakutat tomorrow evening.'

'What a mad thought.'

'But very appealing.'

I took a compass bearing in the direction of the icefall, in case of poor visibility the following day.

The next morning we drank tea until late, thinking we had a short day ahead. Our packs were lighter now, as most of the food was finished. We strode out towards the centre of the glacier and then headed straight down, hoping to get a better view of the icefall below. There is something magical about walking down through fresh sparkling snow, a childlike simplicity of stamping one foot after the other and then staring back along the tracks. As we descended, the air tasted thicker and warmer. It was still serious high mountain country, but we moved with a new freedom, thankful to be off the freezing, steep north face. At this rate, we should be down by midday, I thought.

We paused to put on sunglasses and cream before meandering towards the left side of the icefall. Suddenly we caught sight of menacing cliffs barricading either side of the icefall. Rows of solid green ice the size of high-rise tower blocks.

'Let's hope we can get through this lot quickly,' said Mick dubiously.

I followed an alleyway of snow until halted by a long, wide crevasse. It looked narrower out on the left, but when I got there it was still too wide. I went further, and then jumped across a three-foot gap. Glancing into the void shocked me. It was a huge, cavernous thing, 100 feet down to a sunken snow bridge, and then below that lurked unfathomable blackness. The side walls overhung so steeply that it looked impossible to escape from. It had warmed up considerably, and snow was collecting underneath my crampons. I raised each foot and tapped hard with my axe.

'This place is spooky,' I said, once Mick had made it across the crevasse safely.

'Let's be as quick as we can.'

'I've got a theory, Mick.'

'What's that?'

'I think you should go out in front. The person in front has a bigger chance of falling into a crevasse.'

'You're not selling this well.'

'Part of my mountain guide training was rescuing people out of crevasses. It might be easier to get you out than the other way round.'

'I see what you're saying,' said Mick, unconvinced.

We moved as quickly as we could, but before long our path was blocked by gaping crevasses in every direction. We trudged back uphill, sweating, the sun high in the sky. The splintered walls of the ice cliffs shimmered directly above us.

Mick traversed right and then weaved a good safe line down-hill for almost an hour until a yawning hole appeared. A bridge of blue ice, perhaps four feet wide and four feet thick, arced across to the other side. Mick stepped on to it tentatively, gently prodding at it with his axe as if checking for land mines. We had coils of rope tied off securely across our torsos. It acted as a crude chest harness, but more importantly meant that there was excess rope to use for a rescue if necessary. I had a small mechanical pulley and three prusik knots on the rear of my harness, used to grip the rope when setting up a rescue hoisting system. The crucial point was to keep the rope taut between each other to reduce the shock loading should a fall occur.

Though I understood the theory well, and taught others how to travel safely through such terrain, my heart punched loudly as Mick balanced out towards the centre of the bridge. If that lot collapses, rescue techniques are irrelevant, I thought. I followed on, placing each foot as if treading on eggs, petri-fied. I stared into the evil, monstrous thing, each wall lined with long, clear fangs of ice. Once across, I stood shaking my head, relieved.

The snow was soft underfoot now, and we stopped to strip off our fleece jackets and take a drink. It was water, but with a taste of soup, little grains of noodles in the bottom of the bottle. A pint of lager, that would be good. I put on more face cream and lip salve, and stared back towards the summit.

'It's half past three. We better get a move on, Andy.'

'Time flies when you're enjoying yourself,' I said, trying not to smile, my lips stinging.

I eased my bruised shoulders back into the narrow straps of the rucksack and stood up. My legs felt sore. We had eaten meagre amounts of food for the last seven days and it was beginning to show. A band of thin cloud appeared on the horizon, signalling a change in the weather. I thought I could see the flattening of the lower Cathedral Glacier below, the spot where Kurt said he would pick us up. A long hour of wading through wet, treacle-thick snow brought us there. We dropped our rucksacks. It was all down to Kurt now.

15

Spring

We sat on our rucksacks in the snow, sipping tea. I closed my eyes, listening for the sound of Kurt's engine, trying not to think of how we might escape if he failed to arrive. We had enough gas to melt snow for a few more days, but the food would be finished tomorrow. Mick and I knew from bitter experience that it was getting back down the mountain that mattered. The horror on Changabang had started on the descent, as with so many epic mountaineering tales, from Simpson to Krakauer, Bonatti to Diemberger. What went up did not always come down, and even when it did, sometimes the damage incurred was monstrous.

Just then I heard a faint murmur. 'Listen,' I said, opening my eyes and looking at Mick.

'What?'

'Listen.'

But it was gone. I finished my tea and closed my eyes again. There was no life up here, no sound that could be construed as being a plane. I heard a gentle muttering now, a hint of something, and sat up, slowly swivelling my head left and then right. The muttering became hoarse.

'I think I hear something, a long way away,' said Mick.

We stood up simultaneously, scouring the sky. There was a blatant swelling of sound now, the echo of a wasp caught in a glass jar, and then suddenly a plane appeared over the ridge. People had said that if you wanted to be sure of reaching your mountain and getting back, Kurt was your man, and here he was, banking the Cessna, trying to lose height before dropping down on to the lower Cathedral Glacier.

I worried that we hadn't stopped in the right place, making it more difficult for him to land, but he wouldn't have any of it.

'Hell no, guys. This is exactly the right place,' he said, walking through the snow towards us.

He wore his usual flying uniform: blue denim jeans tucked into nylon gaiters, modest leather boots and a thin fleece, the sort of top I might wear shopping in spring. He took off his gloves and shook our hands, a wonderful, shy grin behind his thick moustache.

'So you made it, there's a thing.'

'We had a few tricky moments, but we did it.'

'I sure thought about you. And the other guys, they're over at base camp, right?'

'Yes. They've climbed a few peaks and they should have packed up some of the stuff. It's Mr Cave's birthday, the man's got a thirst,' Mick said.

I felt a surge of adrenalin once the engine roared into life, the cab vibrating, a gruff baritone instantly drowning out all other sounds. I watched the peak to the right shift as Kurt let the machine glide over the snow. We raced along, a slight undulation throwing us briefly into the air, the shock as we landed back on the ground pounding the struts and jerking us from our seats. I gripped my knees with sweaty palms, then we became airborne and I laughed out loud. Meanwhile Kurt concentrated, scanning the horizon, sporadically glancing at the walls of ice either side of the valley. For the past week, Mick and I had lived with constant uncertainty, having been forced to make continually stressful decisions; now we were merely tourists.

Kurt flicked on the music, it was Dylan again. What a

birthday, I thought: we had climbed the mountain, and now this exhilarating flight. Ahead, thick brushstrokes streaked the horizon, blocking the endless view to the north and east. Suddenly the plane dipped and then rose as we cut our way towards the end of the valley, before swinging left through the familiar notch in the ridgeline. I stared beyond Kurt, again marvelling at how close we were to the walls and ridges. Snow had cleared from the rock slabs and underneath the overhangs, and the remaining snow appeared wetter and heavier, hinting at spring. Once through the notch, we headed west up the South Lowell Glacier towards base camp.

'The guys at base camp have written something in the snow,' said Kurt.

We lost height and then Kurt tilted the wing; we saw Duncan and Chris waving and made out the letters in the deep snow. They read: HAPPY B'DAY.

All I could think of was food, the mere thought of it making me feel faint.

'Did you like your birthday message, Cavey?' boomed Duncan, striding towards us as we opened the door.

'Brilliant,' I said, shaking his hand.

'Sorry about the apostrophe, but we got knackered. Our ascent of the mighty Spunkhorn took its toll,' he said cheekily.

'Did you try Kennedy?' Mick asked.

'There was an enormous crevasse, hundreds of metres long. We just couldn't get over it,' Duncan said. 'We climbed two virgin peaks, though.'

'And we made you a cake,' Chris said, holding out a plate. 'You look like you've lost weight, both of you.'

'Wow, I'm very touched, guys. Can I try a bit now? I am starving.'

'It's malt loaf with jam in the middle, honey and cough sweets on top.'

'How old are you?' asked Duncan.

'Too old for this game. Thirty-four, I think.'

'You're a youngster, Cave, a toddler,' Mick laughed.

We stood there back beneath the north face, the beast we had spent days battling with, eating the curious cake.

'Kurt, is there any chance of flying out a different way, past any steep peaks, stuff for future holidays?' Mick asked.

'We could swing by Alverstone, I guess,' he nodded. 'That's a mean-looking mountain on the west side.'

We loaded half of the equipment into the plane, and then Mick and I squeezed in. The engine rasped and once again we were off and up, circling the glacier, soaking up final views of Mount Kennedy. Alverstone looked like the steep Italian face of Mont Blanc, crenulated ridges of red granite slashed with stripes of ice. I turned around to catch Mick licking his lips and pointing, a man obsessed with mountain adventure. He took shot after shot, dreaming of the holiday beyond the next 12 months of Inland Revenue. Kurt pulled back the controls and we climbed out of the basin and up over a narrow, twisting ridge. Dylan was singing about the wind and snow, as if in the plane with us.

The land opened out now, patches of ice turning gold in the low glancing sun. Behind Mount St Elias a thin layer of low cloud ran towards the horizon, obscuring the ocean; above it a thicker blanket moved in, hinting at change. My pride in our efforts on Mount Kennedy began to fade as I became lost in the landscape. It reminded me a little of the view Dave and I had glimpsed from Fitzroy out towards the Patagonian ice cap. Contemplating such wildness was a humbling experience. The nineteenth-century Patagonian explorer Prichard had been close when he wrote: 'I am inclined to think that the most useful lesson to myself was one that sank deeper and deeper into my mind, I might say heart, with every day lived in these great solitudes – and that was the knowledge of my own ignorance.'

We soared down the Hubbard Glacier now, past thousands of gaping crevasses, like the patterned cracks in a shattered windscreen. It looked nigh on impossible to cross, by foot or ski, though 120 years ago, Abruzzi and his team had dragged their 750lb sledges over similar terrain.

You couldn't help feeling that the story of humanity was but a brief paragraph and your own life an almost invisible mark on the page of this ancient landscape. Of course, scientists now know the landscape is not so enduring. Glaciologists, comparing current aerial photographs of the region with Bradford Washburn's earlier shots, have found that 90 per cent of glaciers in this area have shrunk significantly. Yet, occasionally, the Hubbard Glacier surges, as it did dramatically in 1986. Returning from having dropped off some climbers, Kurt noticed that the glacier had shot out into the bay, cutting off one half of the Russell Fjord. His observations caused alarm among scientists, triggering a rescue operation in which he had a hand to save the sea mammals trapped on the inside of the ice wall. At one point the water level on the inside was 90 feet higher than sea level. Eventually the ice wall burst, causing a monumental and spectacular waterfall.

'She's a beautiful country,' mountain pilot Jack Jefford had said of Alaska. 'But she can be cruel.'

Kurt knew this only too well: his friend and business partner Mike Ivers, a glacier pilot with thousands of flying hours' experience, had been killed in 1992 when he flew his Cessna 207 into a mountainside. Most pilots killed flying in Alaska are inexperienced, but there are exceptions. In 1951, another veteran mountain pilot, Maury King, had vanished in the area we were now flying over. As part of the Snow Cornice Scientific Expedition, King and his passengers, Foresta Wood and her daughter Valerie, left the Seward Glacier, but never made it to Yakutat. King had logged more than 13,000 hours' flying time, nearly half of this on skis. The American and Canadian air forces searched the area thoroughly, but found no trace.

Even around the edges of these mountains, down at sea level, the weather can be atrocious enough. In Yakutat, the wind blows in excess of 40 miles per hour for more than 40 days each year and the town gets between 85 and 130 inches of rainfall. The most violent winds feared by pilots are the Bora winds – known locally along the coast as Williwaw, Takus or Stikine. These are katabatic winds, common by coastal mountain ranges and caused by the temperature differential: cold air descending rapidly towards warmer coastal air masses. More capricious mountain winds exist too, especially near ridges. Local pilot Paul Claus commented that he visualises the air as flowing water: 'Sometimes it flows up, and sometimes down, and sometimes it goes over rocks and turns into whitewater.'

Claus also remarked that although the mountain pilots further north around Denali are superbly skilled, many of them fly a limited number of routes compared to St Elias pilots. Claus, Kurt and Andy Williams over in Whitehorse constantly flew into different locations.

As we approached the end of the sullen, untamed Hubbard Glacier, small dark rivers bled into the Russell Fjord, where squares of ice floated like jewellery thrown in the mud. The narrow fjord curved to the south-east, forming a natural letter 'y'. This area of water was named Disenchanted Bay by the Spanish explorer Malaspina, who had travelled here in 1791 desperately disappointed not to discover the North-West Passage.

We descended, flying above the forest until Yakutat appeared, small but resolute on the long, wild coast.

We had eaten and drunk very little for the past seven days, and now Kurt ordered some whiskies.

'This round is on me,' he said firmly.

'Better celebrate Andy's birthday,' said Mick, raising his glass.

'And a very fine outing,' I said.

We chinked our glasses, swilled down the spirit. The liquid scorched my throat and left me light-headed. But drinking liquor in the Yukon was part of the culture, and Kurt ordered another round for good measure. During the gold rush, locals concocted their own 'hooch' when whisky ran out. The nineteenth-century journalist, Adney, commented: 'It must be very bad, for its manufacture is forbidden by law; they say it will drive a man crazy.' Made from sour dough, or dough and brown sugar, or sugar alone, it was heated in an oil can before peaches or blueberries were added to the clear liquid for taste. It is a fact that many of the miners who did find gold ended up wasting it on booze, gambling and prostitutes. In debt and destitute, many were unable to leave.

'So how did you guys all meet?' Kurt asked.

'I first met Mick in Sheffield. I met him again with Duncan in a bar similar to this; the Clachaig in Glencoe, Scotland.'

'A bar famous for its whisky,' Chris said.

'Mick and Duncan had just been avalanched from the base of a new route they were trying.'

'Yes, that was grim,' Mick said.

'We were lucky to survive that,' said Duncan. 'You had a big black eye, Mick, if I remember.'

'We went back another time and did the climb. "Against all Odds", we called it. You would love it, Andy,' Mick enthused.

'I was in Scotland once. I would love to go back some day and take my daughter with me,' Kurt said.

'How old is she?'

'Ten.'

'You're welcome any time, Kurt,' said Chris.

'In fact we are all spread out between London and Scotland, so you could do a tour, visit us all,' Mick said.

'We might just do that this fall,' Kurt smiled.

Kurt paid for the drinks, which was generous. I couldn't imagine he made a lot of money, especially flying the likes of us into the mountains. He had charged us £300 each, but between us we had made four hour-long flights. Hiring a taxi and driving across London for an afternoon would probably cost more.

When the food arrived we fell silent, the four of us tearing at the steaks like savage dogs. Afterwards, Kurt whisked us off in the Datsun to another bar. I felt he was part of our team now, and I enjoyed learning more of his life as the alcohol stripped away his shyness.

'It must cost a fortune to run a plane,' I said.

'Sure. I mean to begin with I flew under the radar, but that got scary.'

'What do you mean?'

'I started flying with my brother Shawn, but I didn't have any papers. Then this guy from the aviation authorities stopped me on the runway in Seattle. Wanted to see my documents. "Well that might be a problem, sir, I ain't got no licence, I ain't got nothing."'

'What happened?'

'He let it go, but explained the fine was twenty-five thousand dollars and that I better go and get legit.'

'Flying's obviously in the family,' I said.

'My brother Shawn was killed flying last year.'

The guy behind the bar turned up the music.

'Shit. What happened?' asked Duncan.

'He was working in Hawaii. They reckon he lost consciousness from lack of oxygen. Disappeared into the ocean; they never found him, or the plane.'

Kurt finished his drink and I went up to the bar and ordered the next round. Having lost friends in the mountains, I could begin to imagine what the pain of losing a brother would be like. It made me think of my own brother and what he must think of my climbing. I wondered if it made it easier for Kurt being a pilot himself – maybe it was tougher. Either way, I imagined you became addicted to flying, the focus it gave you and the buzz of adjusting to the changing conditions, especially in the small aircraft that these guys flew. The parallels between our worlds were obvious.

Apparently, when flying climbers into the St Elias Mountains, Kurt's friend, the late Mike Ivers, would turn and bellow: 'This is big country, boys!' These pilots were a self-reliant breed, I thought, folk who detested bureaucracy, lovers of freedom and space. Ivers had baulked when the authorities announced they were going to build a fence around Yakutat runway. He hated fences, the very idea of them. A huge, red-haired man, he told people that the reason he'd left Montana was because of 'too many damn fences'. He loved Alaska because it was untamed, the new unexplored frontier.

The bar had filled a bit now. The decor was plain and everyone was dressed the same: denim, cotton T-shirts, a leather jacket or two, a handful of baseball caps, nothing flash. There were no pretensions, but plenty of verve. It reminded me of Saturday nights in bars on Scotland's remote west coast. Kurt was chatting with friends; Mick, Duncan and Chris were playing pool with a local woman.

A giant native Indian guy at the bar leaned over. 'Good trip?' he asked.

'Great,' I said. 'Kurt did a superb job.'

'He's the best, though you wouldn't think it looking at him. He's so modest. How did it go in the mountains?'

'We've climbed in the Himalayas a lot, but the St Elias feels just as serious, more lonely maybe.'

'Not a lot of people out that way.'

He smiled as I grabbed the beers and headed off first to Kurt and then up to the pool table. We played for a couple of hours, our accuracy waning steadily. At around midnight, I noticed Mick was missing. Chris sat down and looked like he was finished. Coming back from the toilet, I met the Indian guy again.

'Around here we have a rule.'

'What's that?' I asked.

'You can drink as much as you like, but don't get drunk.' He pointed to a man lying in a foetal position under a table by the entrance. It was Mick.

'He doesn't get out much these days,' Duncan joked, arriving at the bar.

'Well he can't lay there, friend. You need to move him.'

Kurt suggested that he went and slept in the Datsun, as the bar would be shutting soon anyhow. Mick looked up, startled, his face deathly pale. Following the first ascent of Mount St Elias, the Duke of Abruzzi was resting on his yacht off Yakutat when a visitor arrived. He was shocked to find the duke's face so 'disfigured by venomous bites as to be totally unrecognizable'. 'I have conquaired ze Mount St Elias, but ze mosquitoes, zay have conquaired me,' the duke rejoined. Mick's complexion suggested that he had been defeated by the whisky. He stood up and staggered out towards the car.

The following morning, my forehead pounded furiously. We got up and chatted about when to set off back towards Seattle. If Mick got home early, he could use any remaining holiday time with his family during the summer. I had to finish writing my thesis at the university, and over the summer I'd be working in the Alps. We decided to return to Britain. Duncan and Chris planned to hire a car in Seattle and do some rock-climbing for a week.

The hotel had a jacuzzi two minutes' walk away, and hoping it might refresh us, we paid it a visit. Mick and Chris were forced to stop and vomit in the undergrowth along the way. We sat in our underwear, our brown, peeling faces and necks atop thin white bodies. The water bubbled more and more violently as I pushed the controls. I wanted every jet possible blasting at maximum pelt, but unexpectedly the jacuzzi fell quiet. After days living in nylon thermals, starved of vitamins, our skin was exfoliating, and when the last of the bubbles vanished, a flotsam formed on the surface. I saw a couple in smart swimwear approaching, and tried to restart the jets, desperate to break up the floating crust of dead skin and hair, but the machine stubbornly refused. An unimpressed hotel manager appeared and began skimming off the grey-brown scum with a dredging tool. We apologised and left.

'Ladies and gentlemen, we are flying right over Mount Fairweather,' said the Alaska Airlines captain. 'It's extremely rare to have such clear weather around here, so please take advantage.'

The jet suddenly banked over and we stared directly down on to the summit of Mount Fairweather. The pilot then chucked the aircraft to the other side, for the benefit of the adjacent passengers.

'All Alaskan pilots are bonkers, acrobatics at six hundred miles per hour,' I said.

'He's getting his adrenalin fix,' said Mick, his cheeks still pale.

The following day, an hour or so before landing back in Britain, I felt a tinge of regret that we had left the mountains in such a rush. Spending time in Yakutat could have been interesting too, exploring the coast and the forests. The summit was still fresh in my mind, as well as the exciting trip out in the Cessna. Just the day before, in the tiny Yakutat airport, we had said goodbye to Kurt as the fishermen were proudly checking in their long coolboxes packed with big Alaskan fish. Over time, our trip would become a series of stories, photos and random memories. A thing over all too quickly.

After climbing in Patagonia, Lionel Terray had visited Alaska, making the first ascent of Mount Huntingdon. He, too, lamented having to leave, writing, 'On this proud and beautiful mountain we have lived hours of fraternal, warm and exalting nobility. Here for a few days we have ceased to be slaves and have really been men. It is hard to return to servitude.'

And so, as before, I glided back into normal life, as if I had never left. Making tea in three minutes was wonderful after hour upon hour of melting snow and ice on Mount Kennedy. Trees and flowers were blooming everywhere, and after work Elaine and I enjoyed perfect long evenings climbing on the gritstone edges. In contrast to my return from Changabang three years before, though, I felt buoyant with a zest for life.

At Juneau airport I'd bought a CD called *The Spirit of Alaska*, music and sounds that promised to evoke 'the solitude and grandeur of the untamed Alaskan wilderness'. The banal music was overlaid with exotic bird sounds and the mating call of Arctic seals. It failed to conjure my own experience of Alaska and the Yukon. My CD would have contained the sound of snow sliding past the tent; wind flapping the hood of my jacket; the engine of Kurt's Cessna; Fowler's eccentric tongue; and, of course, the music of Dylan.

16

Kinder

Beyond the stone circle, by the old oak tree, I crouched and then sprang from the back of the cave. The skin on the fingers and palm of my right hand slapped the stone. I hooked my left foot behind a nubbin of rock under the overhang to stop myself swinging wildly and then jumped my left hand out to a faint crease and squeezed. I took a deep breath, lowered out my torso until it was in line with my arms, and then released my feet. I pounced to the big final hold before pressing out both arms and standing up on top of the rock. It was impossible to say how many times I had climbed out of this cave over the years, but it felt as wonderful as ever. It always made me think that even if I ended up being the last man on earth, I would still yearn for this small rock, this desert island stone poem. Sometimes you climbed a beautiful mountain but the climbing itself was tedious. Here the beauty was inseparable from the movement.

Through the branches of the oak tree I saw a man and small girl waving, and I scrambled down the bank to meet them. It was Kurt and Kelsi, visiting from Alaska.

'Hey, great to see you again,' Kurt said, holding out his hand. 'How's the climbing?'

He was clean-shaven and wore a smart shirt, but otherwise

he looked exactly as I remembered him out on the glacier: blue jeans, jacket.

'Not quite as big as your mountains,' I said. 'But the rock is perfect.'

'What sort of rock is it?' asked Kelsi, a bright glint in her eyes.

'Gritstone. They reckon this is what God climbs on, given the choice,' I laughed.

There were about 20 or 30 climbers spread out over the rocks; more climbers than Kurt meets in a year in Yakutat, I thought.

'The Fowler children are demanding to be fed, Andrew,' said Mick, appearing suddenly. We walked back to the cars in a gang and then headed to the café at Elton.

Kurt had decided to take up our offer of places to stay on a countrywide tour. After a few days in London with Duncan and Jacqui, he and Kelsi had visited the Fowlers in Derby. From us, they planned to stop with Chris in Perth before heading to Edinburgh and out to the west coast and the islands. Kurt was eager to visit some of the distilleries.

Elton café, famous for its cakes, was full of walkers and cyclists. Kelsi took lots of photographs with her new digital camera.

'I'm sending them back to my school in Haines,' she explained.

The children exchanged stories, and Kelsi told us how, at weekends, her dad would fly over the mountains from Yakutat to Haines to pick her up. Sometimes they'd fly down to Juneau to watch a movie or do some shopping. People in the café turned around, incredulous at what they were hearing. We spent half an hour saying goodbye to the others, and then Kurt, Kelsi and I weaved our way northwards through small lanes to my house.

Before moving to Alaska, like many kids in Seattle Kurt and his brother Shawn had backpacked in the Cascade Mountains and boated around Puget Sound. He might not have been a mountaineer in the strictest sense, but he shared our need for adventure and space. Many of his climbing clients had become friends. Occasionally, when down in Seattle, he would go and see one of their lectures and join them for a beer afterwards.

Over the years we had been made welcome in people's houses throughout Europe, in Pakistan, India and South America, sometimes by people we barely knew. It was a pleasure to welcome Kurt and Kelsi to our home, new friends from a far-off place.

'What animals do you have here?' Kelsi asked Elaine.

'No grizzly bears, I'm afraid, but squirrels, foxes, badgers and owls,' she said, pointing to a box nailed up high in a sycamore, where a tawny owl now lived.

We walked around the village and swapped stories about our lives. Kurt had left school young, spurning the opportunity to go to university. It was the mid-1970s, and he enlisted with a company supplying drivers to Alaska during the construction of the Alaska pipeline. He received a call one morning, and by the afternoon he was on a plane travelling to the far north. In appalling weather and freezing temperatures, he had had to figure out how to operate enormous trucks, a challenge he had relished.

Back home, I lit a fire.

'This is for you, Andy, a present from Yakutat,' Kurt said. It was a black baseball cap, sporting a robust leather peak.

'Thanks, Kurt, it's brilliant. It'll be great when I'm ski-guiding; keep the snow off my goggles,' I laughed.

'Well, we're being well looked after over here, it's the least we can do.'

'Is that your plane embroidered on the front?' Elaine asked.

Kurt chatted about how he'd bought the Cessna as salvage. It had been on floats originally, but had been flipped over in a lake. He'd paid $75,000 and spent months rebuilding it and fitting the retractable skis allowing him to land in the mountains.

Elaine asked him how he had ended up living in Yakutat and being a pilot. He explained that even as young boys he and Shawn had dreamed of flying planes. After working on the pipeline, he'd settled further north in Big Lake. Shawn had a DC3 and was flying fish from Yakutat and Dry Bay south over the Fairweather Mountains to Juneau. He'd asked Kurt if he wanted to come and help him, which he did for a while. At some point Kurt had met a local girl, Molly, in Yakutat. Although not native Indian by blood, the pair soon married through the native clan system. Things hadn't worked out, though, and Molly and the girls had moved over to Haines Junction.

'I guess I'm still in Yakutat,' he said, smiling.

Sharp and inquisitive, Kelsi bombarded us with questions about life in Britain: what music we listened to; what TV we watched; how old the house was; what we liked to eat. In the kitchen before we had dinner, I suggested to Elaine that Kurt and I might go off to the local pub for a couple of pints later. Elaine looked flabbergasted.

'Kelsi is lovely, but she's a livewire. She isn't going to want to sleep for hours; listen to her jabbering,' she said.

She had a valid point: it was a selfish thought and we had plenty to drink in the house anyhow. Plus, I remembered the state Kurt and I had got into the last time we'd been out together, in Yakutat. After dinner we sat in the lounge in front of a roaring fire and I opened a bottle of Laphroaig.

'Do you burn coal?' queried Kurt.

'Wood mainly, coal occasionally,' said Elaine. 'Andy worked as a coal miner, you know.'

'Really?'

'Forty minutes up the road,' I said. 'Most of my family worked there, but it's all closed down now.'

'What do people do?'

'It's difficult. Many of the older men lacked confidence initially to begin new jobs. Which is odd when you think that underground on the coalface they dealt with the unknown every day,' I said. 'It was a dirty and dangerous job, but many of them got a great sense of pride from it, as well as money.'

'Your job sounds incredible, Kurt,' said Elaine.

'You don't have anyone telling you what to do; I like that, plus the work is varied.'

'Andy mentioned your brother's accident,' she said.

'Shawn was an extremely skilled pilot. They don't really know what happened. He'd taken some skydivers up and was heading back down and just went straight into the ocean.'

I put another log on the fire and poured out more whisky.

'Sounded like Mick and you had a tough time out in India a couple of years ago,' Kurt said after a pause.

'Yes, it took me a long time to get over losing a friend like that. No climb is worth a life. In the mountains you only have to make a small mistake at the wrong time and you can be punished. Changabang taught me that.'

'You've been climbing for a long time, right?'

'Seventeen years,' I said. 'Sometimes I wonder what I would have done with my life if I hadn't discovered climbing.'

'You have plans?'

'We want to travel through America climbing,' Elaine said. 'Oregon, Utah and California.'

'Yes, we're looking forward to that. I love the places that climbing takes us, and the people you end up meeting. I've seen photos of areas in China that look amazing, phenomenal unclimbed mountains, wild places. Patagonia, too, I definitely want to go back there,' I enthused.

It was getting late, but Kurt and Kelsi showed no signs of tiring. I stoked up the fire, finished my whisky and we left them to it.

The next day we drove over the moors, stopping from time to time so that Kelsi could get some photos. Later, at the railway station, Kurt and I shook hands.

'It's been great to see you again,' I said.

'You're always welcome in Yakutat,' he said, with his wonderful smile.

'Bye, Andy,' said Kelsi, waving.

'There's more space up in Scotland,' I said. 'You'll have a great time.'

They walked off and soon disappeared into the crowd.

The following Sunday morning, Elaine and I walked up to Stanage Edge and climbed easy classic routes with minimal equipment. The conditions were ideal and I enjoyed the lightness of climbing without a rucksack in just a T-shirt. As the day wore on, the cliff filled, until queues formed at the base of some of the more popular routes. The climbing was so good, and being just 12 miles outside of Sheffield, you had to accept it would be busy. Nevertheless, it was far from a wilderness experience.

'I haven't seen so many people here for ages,' said Elaine.

'I know. It's such a gorgeous day for this time of year,' I replied.

I looked over at Kinder, brooding in the distance. That was the place to be for a quiet climb. The long walk in, strange, granular rock and tough grades put many people off.

Later that week, I drove out of the city, past rows of pensive students marching to and from lectures. I thrashed the car uphill past the hospital and then out along the Manchester road, cutting through bright green fields down to the reservoir. It wasn't a big city, but still it felt good to escape.

I parked up and strode into the cool of the woods, startled birds darting in the darkness. Beyond, the path split and I took the one less travelled that followed the river and then twisted up on to the moor until opposite the shooting cabins. When the path stopped, I dropped into a narrow gully and up the other side, crunching through dead ferns. The moor flattened out now, becoming spongy, the thick bristle of heather chafing my ankles as I bounded towards the bizarrely shaped rocks, the envy of Rodin and Moore. Ahead, a rabbit sat tall, his large, distrustful eyes scouring the horizon until my footsteps alarmed a grouse and he bolted like a hunted man. I thought of that first trip to Kinder with Rhino and the twins; the underage drinking in Edale and getting lost in the mist. The place had given me so much pleasure over the years.

There were no paths at all now, just the occasional tiny water-filled hollow where silt and rainwater had rushed down the moor and collected. I stopped by a patch of grass below a gorgeous wall of rock, generously laden with large holds, a 20-foot-high stone Swiss cheese, perfect for warming up the shoulders. Looking out, I noticed that, other than the shooting cabins, there was no sign of civilisation. Sheffield was hidden, Manchester down on the other side. In fact you saw more of Manchester and Sheffield from here at night when their lights dyed the sky ochre. I ate a sandwich and then put on my rock shoes and chalk bag and set off, aping up the first thing I saw. On top, the hint of a breeze blew from the west. I stared around, alert to any movement; I'd still never seen a short-eared owl.

For an hour I climbed over the boulders, swinging from pocket to sloping shelf, hardly noticing the roughness of the stone biting and scratching at my skin. I finished my sandwiches and moved along to where the rocks became higher. I saw a square wall above a dangerous jumble of boulders and heather. I could see it had holds but they looked marginal and a fall here would wreck an ankle at the very least, which could be serious in a place like this. I hadn't got a mobile phone, not that there was likely to be any reception up here anyhow. Either way it would be a mammoth crawl back to the car. I walked on and climbed a series of shorter walls, requiring balance and subtle footwork. The friction on the rock was excellent, and I wandered back until I was beneath the wall and decided to give the first few moves a try; I didn't have to do the whole thing.

The first handhold was decent, two joints of the knuckles deep, allowing me to move my feet into shallow scoops. The vertical wall looked blank above, except for a three-inch strip of iron rugosity. I reached up and pulled at it, a small fragment breaking, like a piece of rotten, rusting tin can.

I swept the hold with my fingers and then pulled again. It seemed OK. I threw my right foot up to a large pebble and then stood up, slightly off balance. Staring down, I could see I was directly above the most menacing sharp boulder. A few feet higher I spied a tiny pocket. If I could use that, it might be possible, but I had hung too long from the small finger holds and my arms were pumped. I climbed back down, took my shoes off and glugged some water.

I had made a pact with the few friends I'd been up here with not to divulge what we had climbed, so that it would remain a quiet little haven. We gave things names among ourselves but never wrote anything down and didn't assign grades. We came here for solitude and the views mainly. This attractive wall had got me hooked. It might never get climbed again, but that didn't matter. I fancied doing it just for the hell of it.

I reached the rusty fragile hold more quickly this time and continued up towards the small pocket. I jabbed my right middle finger into the half-inch-deep hole and searched with my left hand. The rock was blank and I felt unbalanced. My arms began to tire. I moved my feet down, removed my finger from the pocket. I stood on a pebble, but felt it crumble. I held a small edge with my right hand and hooked my left middle finger into the pocket and stood up. At full stretch, I crept my fingers on to a bump in the rock. It was marginal but easier than trying to go back down. Fully committed now, I trusted my weight to it and then clawed at the heather, managing to place my foot on to a decent hold before standing up.

On top I lay back, intoxicated, and closed my eyes. What a glorious thing to do, pointless but so much fun. It was a long while since I had climbed something like that alone. At one time, I had soloed quite a lot on the gritstone edges and occasionally in the mountains. I still enjoyed the buzz of climbing, but these days I valued the camaraderie and the safety of doing it with a friend.

After our epic on Changabang it had become harder to justify taking big risks to friends, family and myself. It wasn't just Brendan's death that had been so disturbing, but the realisation that the avalanche in India very nearly wiped us all out. You can strive to minimise the risk, but you can't eliminate it completely. Maybe that was what I had been forced to accept.

I had always relied on the quiet inner voice in the mountains, a sort of risk barometer: Changabang had shaken my faith in it. Perhaps if I had returned to the big mountains sooner, as

Mick and Steve had done, I might have got over the trauma sooner. But I had got there eventually, and Mount Kennedy had been a wonderful adventure. There was something incredibly compelling about pushing yourself into the unknown, with a good friend. You had to commit to each other and to the mountain, but afterwards you were left with such clarity. It wasn't that I despised routine everyday life, far from it, but being up high in the elements replenished my spirit. For me, that was reason enough to travel and climb in remote inhospitable lands.

Abruptly, something tore a hole in my calm. A massive jet approached, relatively close to the ground. They circled up here sometimes, killing time, waiting for a slot to land at Manchester airport. The plane rumbled overhead for a couple of minutes, the silence gone. The sky was a busy place nowadays, I thought. Recently, Dave Hesleden had told me that direct daily flights had begun to El Calafate in Patagonia. Inevitably that would encourage more people to visit the Fitzroy area, but the vicious winds would mean that the summits never became crowded. In the wild St Elias Mountains, I was convinced that the prolonged snowstorms would prevent the place becoming too popular. I was glad of that.

Epilogue

On 16 July 2001, Americans Bill Pilling and Andy Selters started climbing the 6000-foot north buttress of Mount Kennedy in the heart of the St Elias Mountains, Yukon. The pair had been dropped off below the peak six days earlier by ace mountain pilot Kurt Gloyer. Experienced mountaineers Pilling, 43, and Selters, also 43, from Bishop, California, were compelled to try what had been deemed by some mountaineers as 'the most beautiful mountain climb in the world'. They planned to climb in lightweight alpine style, the route having been climbed in this way for the first time the previous year by a British party.

Initially the climb went well. After 20 hours of climbing, the pair cut into the ice, clearing a place to sleep. They were tired and dehydrated, but pleased that they had completed the first half of the route.

After a rest day they continued, bivouacking as it got dark below a jutting roof in the middle of a 500-foot black diorite rock band. This comprised the steepest part of the climb. Selters woke the next morning to find he couldn't move his right foot. A slip the day before had pinched a nerve in his back, aggravating an old injury. They agreed that Pilling would take responsibility for leading out the rope.

The following day, however, Pilling admits he made a

route-finding error which led to the pair making an abseil. They bivouacked again and then moved up easier slopes before spending one more night below the summit. They didn't sleep much, a westerly wind battering their tent with spindrift. On the top, they enjoyed spectacular views, but their anxiety grew as they watched cirrus clouds building to the south. The climbers had started with food for six days and this was the sixth day. They had also decided to leave the satellite phone at base camp, deeming it too bulky to carry. It was a decision they would come to regret.

They started to descend the south side of the mountain in deteriorating weather. Through gaps in the cloud, the Cathedral Glacier below them looked a maze of gaping crevasses and fragile snow bridges as last winter's snows receded. Eventually, in the mist, they found a flat place on the edge of the glacier and got into the tent. That night it started to snow, thick, quiet flakes. They had virtually no food and two gas canisters left, one only half full.

'For years, I'd had a nightmare that one day I'd get trapped on the backside of one of these big, remote mountains,' Pilling said later.

The following afternoon the storm slowed, so the climbers decided to move out on to the glacier and up into a basin at around 12,000 feet, directly below the col between Mount Alverstone and Mount Hubbard. When it cleared, they planned to climb over Mount Alverstone to avoid the ugly glacier below and make the eight-mile trek back to base camp for the rendezvous with the pilot. For Selters, walking was difficult, his back still hurt and he had to lean to one side to relieve the pain.

Without visibility, and with wet snow still falling, they had no choice but to stay in the tent the next day. Pilling began to fret, but Selters reminded him of the time he had spent eight days without food in the Himalayas. They put snow in their water bottles and then placed them inside their sleeping bags, to let their body heat begin melting it.

'We drank just enough to keep our kidneys functioning and

to stave off the cold, no more than a pint each per day,' Pilling says.

The weather remained poor, rain and snow beating against the tent. They were slowly starving.

'I felt my eye sockets and hip bones grow more prominent,' Selters recalls.

They had no contact with the outside world. On an earlier expedition to the Fairweather Mountains, Pilling remembered seeing Gloyer and his brother flying over them in their DC3, taking fish to Juneau. But the nearest flight path was 60 or 70 miles away, over Yakutat, and they saw and heard nothing.

Growing more and more desperate as they remained trapped, Pilling scratched a will into the handle of his climbing partner's knife.

'I carved the names of people I loved, members of my family along with a couple of ex-girlfriends, and wrote how I wanted my money dividing.'

On 25 July, the eleventh day since leaving base camp, they went outside and stamped a plea for help in the snow, asking for food and fuel. They figured that if a plane did pass, it might at least be able to drop supplies.

The next day was Thursday, the day Gloyer was due to pick them up from base camp. Pilling had flown many times with Gloyer. He knew his routine, knew that he preferred to fly early or late, when there was often less cloud. That morning the weather was still bad and Gloyer didn't show.

'If Kurt comes today, it will be tonight,' Pilling told Selters.

By the afternoon, the weather had improved and patches of blue appeared overhead. The men knew that Gloyer was familiar with the Cathedral Glacier; and that he'd dropped climbers off on this side of the mountain before. Also, they had left a proposed itinerary of their route with the Canadian Park Services.

At around 5 p.m. they heard the faint sound of an engine. Pilling remembers looking at his watch and guessing it was Gloyer looking for them.

'We reckoned that once he found the empty base camp he'd come and check this side of the mountain.'

They were right. Gloyer flew up the South Lowell Glacier, landed the Cessna and looked around the climbers' base camp. Realising there was nobody inside the tent, he took off again, eventually flying over the ridge between Mount Kennedy and Hubbard.

Pilling and Selters began waving their jackets furiously. After days of fear worming its way deeper into their minds, the echo of the engine kindled their hope. Gloyer landed uphill, 300 feet above their tent, and got out to meet them.

The two men hastily rolled their gear into the tent fabric and dragged it towards the plane, elated to see him.

Pilling remembers Gloyer asking them if they had much kit, and picking up the tent, saying it was OK.

They threw the gear in and then got in themselves. Selters sat in the rear, planning what he would eat first when he got back. Pilling had seen the skill and hard work of these pilots many times before, and he prided himself on being an efficient passenger. This time, though, he was so exhausted he forgot to push the chrome door handle anti-clockwise to lock it. Gloyer noticed, reached across and did it for him.

Gloyer increased the revs and then set the plane off down the steep slope. The time was about 6.15 p.m.

'I pulled my waist belt and shoulder straps as tight as I could,' says Pilling.

The plane went fast to begin with, but then the slope levelled and it lost speed. The skis chattered on wind drifts in the frozen ground, rattling the whole plane. The Cessna gained speed once again, but still it didn't leave the ground. The glacier began undulating and the machine rode in and out of the dips. Looking out of the window, Pilling now realised that they were travelling over bridges spanning huge crevasses. The dips became sharper.

We're either going to make it very soon, or this is it, Pilling remembers thinking.

The Aviation Investigation Report later recorded: 'The aircraft eventually came into contact with a large drift of compacted snow. The propeller and the skis separated from the aircraft and were found in this location. Shortly after contacting this drift, the aircraft nosed over and fell into the next open crevasse.'

'There was nothing but white in front of us and then the white began to darken and darken and darken. I remember snow crystals melting under pressure against the windscreen, and then I lost consciousness,' Pilling says.

When Pilling regained consciousness he was upside down. He looked outside and thought it was cloudy. Then he realised he was in a crevasse.

He knew that he had to get out. His fingers fumbled for the buckles and straps, and then groped for the chrome handle. He crawled out on to the ice dazed and confused.

Once outside, he could see that the Cessna was belly up, stuck on a sloping snow bridge that spanned the width of the crevasse. 'I had to keep licking blood off my glasses,' Pilling remembers. Above, smooth vertical walls, 80 feet high, rose towards a narrow crack of light. He noticed that on one side, a big cornice jutted from the lip of the crevasse.

All the surrounding snow was doused in aviation fuel. An electrical component whirred in the plane's engine; otherwise it was completely still. Meanwhile, Selters, who was completely trapped in the rear, heard Pilling rustling and then opening his door.

'Bill, are you OK?' Selters recalls shouting.

But Pilling didn't appear to hear him. While Pilling was outside, Selters became aware that Gloyer's breathing had stopped.

'I couldn't see Bill, but it was obvious from his lack of memory and confused talk that he had a head injury,' wrote Selters afterwards.

Slowly the fog inside Pilling's mind began to clear. He went back into the plane and moved a few things, but became distracted and soon left. He went outside and started uncoiling a rope, convinced he could climb out of the crevasse.

Upside down, hanging from his straps and totally trapped, Selters was utterly desperate. An orange duffel bag and an ice tool pinned him to his seat. Blood seeped across his eye then along his forehead. Each time he tried to move, his back exploded in pain. Then he heard Pilling moving again outside. He yelled for help, but Pilling was self-absorbed.

Selters waved his foot and noticed a space above him: this gave him hope. He levered his arm from under the ice axe, pulling with all the strength he could muster, grunting, straining. He felt himself shifting by millimetres. It was the hardest thing he had ever done, but somehow it worked. He began to move, then suddenly he was free. He lay still, gasping, before crawling towards the door.

Selters saw that the snow bridge the plane had crashed on to was solid, but a wide slit led deeper into the abyss below. The steep walls meant that climbing out would be a daunting prospect, but he also knew that their only chance of surviving the night was to stay in the crevasse: on the glacier, they would have no shelter. He managed to persuade Pilling to come back inside the plane, where they could try and find somewhere to sit out the night.

It was at this point that Pilling asked about Gloyer.

'Kurt didn't make it,' Selters told him.

By now, they could see little. The watery light was fading. Both men had sustained serious injuries and were cold and desperately thirsty. They found a water bottle but then lost it in the chaos of the cockpit.

'We had a stove, but were too afraid to light it because of the aviation fuel,' Pilling says. 'We got out the two-person sleeping bag. It had been cut in the crash and feathers floated everywhere, sticking to the blood on our faces.'

They sat inside the plane, 'a sloping shell of hard metal with brutal seams and knife-like bolts', describes Selters. 'The pain in my back quickly grew into a terrific roar.'

'I knocked the scab on my forehead and blood oozed on to my face, so I took off my glasses and licked them clean,' Pilling recalls.

The men huddled together waiting for morning. Pilling seemed less confused now, and told Selters he was sure people would come looking for them once the authorities realised that Gloyer's plane was missing.

They just prayed that snow would not fall to cover their tracks and that rescuers would find signs of where they were. In fact, at 10.05 that night, Les Hartley of Gulf Air Taxi in Yakatut notified the coast guard that one of his planes had failed to return from a trip to Mount Kennedy.

On the morning of 27 July, the Canadian Park Rescue helicopter scoured the Cathedral Glacier for clues. The crew found the letters in the snow and, lower down, tracks that they initially thought must have been from the Cessna taking off, but nothing else. Suddenly one of the team spotted the propeller sticking out of the ice, two of the blades forming a vertical V. Swooping forward, they saw the aircraft in the bottom of a deep, narrow crevasse and caught sight of a tiny hand waving out of a window.

The rescue team came back with ropes and stretchers, lowering a man down into the crevasse. They took Pilling out first, and helped him stagger to the helicopter. Then they brought out Selters on a stretcher, before returning later for the pilot's body. Close by, on a small glacier circled by jagged peaks, a group of black Hawk helicopters squatted in a semicircle, nose in. In turn, the rescuers strapped the casualties into separate helicopters. Then they started the rotors, a deafening eerie thud, and flew out of the mountains.

Andy Selters and Bill Pilling both made good recoveries and still enjoy the mountains. Andy Parkin and Dave Hesleden continue to pioneer difficult new routes in Scotland, the Alps and beyond. Leo Houlding has been base jumping for a number of years now in between climbing hard, bold routes. Mick Fowler's appetite for establishing first ascents in the

Himalayas is undiminished. In February 2008 I returned to Patagonia and reached the summit of Fitzroy.

Kurt Gloyer is sadly missed by all who knew him: fellow pilots, mountaineers and the local community in which he played such a central role.

Author's Note

Many people have helped me to complete this book. Firstly I would like to thank my climbing partners, in particular Mick Fowler, Dave Hesleden, Leo Houlding and Andy Parkin. The British Mountaineering Council and the Mount Everest Foundation provided financial support for the expeditions to Patagonia and the Yukon and we are extremely grateful for this. I would like to thank David Udberg of Lowe Alpine-Asolo (UK) for his continued support.

I would also like to thank Jenny Lowe, Doug Chabot, Jack Tackle, Nick Lewis and Brian Hall for helping me piece together the history of Mount Kennedy. I am particularly indebted to St Elias pioneer Bill Pilling, who gave so much of his time and shared his experiences of Mount Kennedy. Andy Selters, too, was kind enough to give a detailed description of events on the same expedition. Special thanks are due to Kelsi Gloyer of Haines Junction, and Les Hartley, mountain pilot of Yakutat, for helping verify important details. My Norwegian friends Trym Sæland and Sindre Bo have provided information about the Kjerag, Lysefjord.

I would like to thank all the people who have provided photographs, and James Nightingale at Hutchinson for unearthing archival images. Yvonne Sibbald, librarian at the Alpine Club Library, London, has been extremely helpful. Javier

Sepúlveda kindly translated passages of the Spanish texts. Val Randall made some excellent suggestions in the first two chapters and showed enthusiasm for the project as a whole.

Three people in particular have been instrumental in bringing this book to fruition. My agent Euan Thorneycroft, of A.M. Heath, has been incredibly supportive of this project from the outset and given solid advice along the way. Tony Whittome, climber and lover of wild places, and my editor at Random House, has been encouraging throughout and allowed my voice to flourish, before his objective, expert eye made invaluable suggestions, in particular regarding the shape and continuity of the material. Without question, the biggest thanks must go to my wife Elaine. She has given her time and spirit generously, scouring each line with her scrupulous literary mind. She made countless crucial suggestions and chatted through ideas at length with unerring passion. I am eternally grateful, thank you. Needless to say, any faults that remain are strictly my own.

Thin White Line draws on the books and articles listed below.

Adney, Tappan, *The Klondike Stampede* (New York, 1899)

Agostini, Alberto R.P. de, *Andes Patagónicos* (Buenos Aires, 1941)

Allen, Benedict, *The Faber Book of Exploration* (London, 2002)

Aviation Investigation Report A01W0186, *Transportation Safety Board of Canada*, 26 July 2001

Azema, M. A., *The Conquest of Fitzroy*, trans. Morin (London, 1957)

Boas, Franz, *Indian Myths and Legend from the North Pacific Coast of America* (Vancouver, 2002)

Bracken, James, *Che Boludo!* (Bariloche, 2005)

Burton, Pierre, *Klondike: The Last Great Goldrush* (Toronto, 1958)

Buscaini, Gino, and Metzeltin, Silvia, *Patagonia: Tierra Magica Para Viajeros Y Alpinistas*, trans. M.J.L. Chollet (Madrid, 2000)

Childs, Herbert, *El Jimmy: Outlaw of Patagonia* (Philadelphia, 1936)

Claus, M. Naske, and Slotnick, Herman E., *Alaska: A History of the 49th State* (Norman, 1994)

Coyle, Daniel, 'The First Law of Gravity', *Outside*, August 1998

Day, Beth, *Glacier Pilot: The story of Bob Reeve and the flyers who pushed back Alaska's frontiers* (New York, 1957)

Diamond, Jared, *Guns, Germs, and Steel* (New York, 1999)

Fowler, John, '"Feurland", a piece of Falklands history returns to Germany', *MercoPress*, Stanley, 6 April 2006

Fowler, Mick, *On Thin Ice* (London, 2005)

Holdich, T.H., 'The Patagonian Andes', *The Geographical Journal*, No. 2, February 1904

Ibaibarriga, Mercedes, 'La aldea más insólita de Argentina', *El Mundo*, Spain, 30 July 2005

Jennifer Speake (ed.), *Literature of Travel and Exploration: An Encyclopaedia* (London, 2003)

Juneau Daily News Online, 30 July 2001

Karl, Reinhard, 'By a Hair', *Mountain*, No. 87, September/October 1987

Kennedy, Robert F., Washburn, Bradford, and Whittaker, James W., 'Canada's Mount Kennedy', *National Geographic*, July 1965

Litvachkes, Roberto, *Gunther Plüschow* (Buenos Aires, 2006)

Madsen, Andreas, *La Patagonia Vieja, Relatos en el Fitzroy* (Buenos Aires, 1948)

Markham, Beryl, *West With the Night* (New York, 1942)

McMillan, Alan D., and Yellowhorn, Eldon, *First Peoples in Canada* (Vancouver, 2004)

Moore, Terris, and Andrasko, Kenneth, 'Shining Mountains, Nameless Valleys: Alaska and the Yukon, Part I', *Alpine Journal* 1976 (Part II 1978; Part III 1979)

Musters, George C., *At Home with the Patagonians* (London, 1871)

Neate, Gill, *Mountaineering in the Andes* (London, 1994)

Nisbet, Andrew, 'Beinn Bhàn: Recent Developments', in *Cold Climbs*, ed. Ken Wilson and John Barry (London, 1991)

Parnell, Ian, 'Victors of the Unwinnable', *Alpinist* 16, Summer 2006

Parrish, Michael, 'Enjoying Alaska at a glacial pace', *LA Times*, 21 July 2002

Potter, Jean, *The Flying North* (San Francisco, 1986)

Prichard, H.Hesketh, *Through the Heart of Patagonia* (London, 1902)

Roberts, Jack, 'Kennedy Diary', *Canadian Alpine Journal*, 1997

Saint-Exupéry, Antoine de, *Night Flight*, trans. Cate (London, 1971)

Scott, Chic, *Pushing the Limits: The Story of Canadian Mountaineering* (Calgary, 2002)

Selters, Andy, 'Ecstasy into Agony', *Climbing*, No. 215, September 2002

Selters, Andy, *Ways to the Sky: A Historical Guide to North American Mountaineering* (Golden, 2004)

Slingsby, Cecil W., *Norway: The Northern Playground* (Edinburgh, 1904)

Terray, Lionel, *Conquistadors of the Useless*, trans. Sutton (London, 1963)

Theroux, Paul, *The Old Patagonian Express* (London, 1979)

Topham, Harold, 'An Expedition to Mount St Elias, Alaska', *The Alpine Journal*, 1889

Wallis, Roger, 'The St Elias Mountains: A Preliminary Survey of the Unclimbed Peaks over 3600m', *Canadian Alpine Journal*, 1992

Whillans, Don, and Omerod, Alick, *Portrait of a Mountaineer* (London, 1971)

Of the writing concerning life in Patagonia during the nineteenth century, I thoroughly enjoyed Musters' *At Home with the Patagonians*, which provides a fascinating insight into the daily lives of Patagonian Indians. Childs' book, *El Jimmy*, is a rich portrait of a remarkable character. Buscaini and Metzeltin give an excellent overview of Agostini's explorations among people and mountains in Tierra del Fuego and Patagonia. Unfortunately, none of Agostini's 22 books have been translated into English to my knowledge. For a meticulous history of mountain exploration in the Andes generally, Gill Neate's *Mountaineering in the Andes* is essential. Azema's account of the first ascent of Fitzroy in 1952 is a superb read and so much more than a 'classic' expedition book, as is Slingsby's narrative, recounting his Norwegian adventures.

Alaska, by Claus and Slotnick, contains an invaluable critical bibliographical essay which succinctly surveys the plethora of material relating to Alaska's cultural, political and economic history. Though essentially concerned with mountaineering, Moore and Andrasko's series of articles provide insight into early explorers of the St Elias Mountains and accompanying coastline. Tappan Adney is considered one of the more reliable journalists of the Yukon gold rush and his book is packed with wonderful detail. The failed attempt to climb Mount St Elias reported by Harold Topham is excellent. For a detailed historical overview of mountaineering in the St Elias look no further than Chic Scott's *Pushing the Limits*, and to see how achievements here fit into a wider framework of North American mountaineering, do consult Andy Selters' impressive book.

Jean Potter's *The Flying North* is perhaps what inspired me the most to write *Thin White Line*. This small book is a vital record of pioneering aviation in Alaska and the result of much fieldwork at a crucial point in history. I do not know of a similar work drawing together the disparate but related experiences of pioneering pilots in South America, though work by Saint-Exupéry and more recently Litvachkes is superb.

Index

INDEX